A History of the Great Western Railway
2. The Thirties, 1930–39

A History of the
Great Western Railway
2. The Thirties, 1930-39

Peter Semmens, M.A., C.Chem., F.R.S.C., M.B.C.S., M.C.I.T.

London
GEORGE ALLEN & UNWIN
Boston   Sydney

First published in 1985
Reprinted 1986, 1987, 1988
Reprinted 1990 by Studio Editions Ltd. by
arrangement with George Allen & Unwin.

Studio Editions Ltd.
Princess House, 50 Eastcastle Street,
London W1N 7 AP, England

Printed in Great Britain by Biddles Ltd.
Guildford, Surrey.

Contents

List of Illustrations and Tables

Tables

I
Introduction

1. GWR monogram used from 1934 onwards instead of the coat of arms.

In the first volume of this series I outlined the pre-history of the Western Group which was formed under the Railway Act of 1921, and then recounted the major events of the 1920s as they affected the resulting enlarged Great Western Railway Company. The difficult early years of the 1920s had been weathered by the British railways generally, and, in spite of the General Strike of 1926, the end of the decade saw traffic and revenue rising once more. The Wall Street crash of October 1929, however, was to plunge the developed world into an economic depression of greater severity than anything experienced before, and, as always, the railway companies' fortunes were closely linked to the general economic prosperity of the country whose industries they served. We thus need to chart the British economic scene during the 1930s in order to set the Great Western Railway's achievements in that decade in context.

Unemployment in 1927 had briefly sunk below the one million mark, representing at that time just under 9 per cent of the insured workforce. Seasonal fluctuations kept the figure around the 10 per cent level over the following two years, but the effect of the Great Depression was to double unemployment in little over a year. In early 1933 there were just under three million unemployed, representing some 23 per cent of those insured. The following year saw an appreciable improvement to about the two million level. During the summer of 1937 there was a further appreciable fall to less than 10 per cent, but this was transitory and the level rose again until the country geared itself to face the threat of German aggression in 1939. The national rearmament campaign, with the construction of the shadow factories throughout the country, saw a dramatic fall in unemployment in the first half of 1939, with the railways similarly starting to prepare themselves for the coming conflict.

One of the effects of the economic recession was to reduce the cost of living, which was still, throughout the 1930s, being quoted in the form of a percentage above the July 1914 level. The

9

summer of 1933 saw the index reach its lowest level between the wars, the average for that year only being 40 per cent above the 1914 figure, compared with 64 per cent in 1929. There was a slight rise over the next few years, but the rearmament campaign saw a marked increase in the index, which then jumped by no less than 10 per cent over the 1914 figure between the first two months of hostilities in 1939.

Throughout the 1930s the railways were, by and large, continuing with existing technology, but rival forms of transport were beginning to develop in size and sophistication. The number of cars on our roads doubled in ten years, from just under one million in 1929, and, while there was only a 50 per cent increase in goods vehicles, their threat to the railways in terms of haulage capabilities was proportionally much greater. The increasing traffic on the roads and its social effects caused great national concern, particularly the rapidly rising accident rate, and the 1930s were to see various moves to regulate road vehicles and their drivers in one way or another. Quantity licensing was introduced for lorries, while other new requirements, such as speed limits and driving tests, were to affect all road users, private and commercial. As a result of all this legislation, and the imposition of a higher tax on petrol to encourage home production, the railways were cushioned to some extent from the build-up of competition, but were still forced to launch their 'Fair Deal' campaign during 1939.

Coal production in Britain increased by about 20 per cent compared with the lowest level in the depression, to a peak of 240 million tons in 1937, but this was substantially below the output achieved in 1929. Iron and steel, the other traditional heavy haul for the railways, was somewhat more buoyant. The production of iron ore nearly doubled between 1933 and 1937, with steel production similarly rising by over 80 per cent during the same period. The 1937 output levels in both these cases were higher than they had been before the Wall Street crash. On the passenger side, the depression left the passenger journeys on the main line railways as a whole relatively unscathed, with a drop of less than 10 per cent between 1929 and 1933. By 1937 the total was appreciably more than the 1929 figure, but between the separate railway companies there were appreciable variations. The Southern Railway, with its programme of suburban electrification, achieved an almost unbroken annual increase right through the depression, and by 1937 was nearly 20 per cent up on 1929. It follows, therefore, that the other companies' performances could not have been as good as the country-wide average, and all their 1937 figures were in fact down on the corresponding ones for 1929. The LMS came nearest to regaining its market, but the GWR experienced a 10 per cent reduction over this period. There was a continuing increase in seaside holidays during the 1930s, which exacerbated the Summer Saturday peaks, both by road and rail. I have vivid recollections of the chaos suffered by road traffic in Exeter during the mid-1930s, when as a youngster I would overtake on foot enormous queues of cars waiting to get through the Exe Bridge bottleneck. Great efforts were made by the city authorities to deal with these peak flows, but, as we will see later, the Great Western was ahead of the road authorities with the provision of new facilities to cope with this holiday traffic. The railway's efforts were a continuation of the process started in the 1920s, as discussed in my earlier volume, and the experience gained in handling vast numbers of people was to enable the railways to play such an important part in the evacuation of civilians from London at the beginning of World War II.

Mention was made in the earlier volume of the financial inducements made by the government to the railways at the end of the 1920s to stimulate trade and industry. The relief of rates was followed by the Development (Loan Guarantees and Grants) Act of 1929, and the advantage taken of the latter by the Great Western was to bring about numerous changes to the system which still make their contribution to the railway we use today. Some of the more ambitious schemes embarked on with Government help, however, were to be thwarted by the declaration of war in 1939 and never revived.

With the difficult economic conditions and the falling cost of living, it was understandable that the railways should seek to reduce their labour costs during the 1930s. Reference was made in my earlier volume to the agreement for a 2½ per cent reduction in wages and salaries introduced in 1928. As a result of trade union pressure, the reduction was terminated in May 1930 after operating for not quite two years. At this stage of the depression the railways clearly wished for the continuation of such an arrangement, and in the light of the union opposition they referred the matter to the National Wages Board. As a result, the original rate of reduction was restored in March 1931, together with a further 2½ per cent for the higher paid (those receiving over £100 per annum or 40 shillings a week). Over the following few years there was considerable negotiation on wage levels generally, with little change overall, but from the summer of 1936 the reductions were halved and finally abolished a year later. There were two general wage rises in 1939, which saw the minimum weekly rate rise from 42s (£2.10) to 45s (£2.25) and then 47s (£2.35). So the railway employees, like those in many other walks of life, had taken a cut in wages or salaries during the years of the depression, but it must be remembered that between 1928 and 1933 the retail cost of living index fell by over 15 per cent, so for those with jobs the degree of belt-tightening must not have been too great, although standards of living were not particularly cosy in those days. Over the same period the dividends on the Great Western's ordinary shares fell by 40 per cent (and disappeared completely on the LMS and LNER), so it would appear that, by the standards of the time, the railway workforce was not unduly penalised during the depression.

Another significant development during the 1930s was the increasing degree of cooperation between the four rival railway companies. In addition to the continuing activities of the Railway Clearing House in the fields of technical and commercial standardisation, various other significant developments took place. There were joint publicity schemes of various sorts, the simplest example being the posters for Devon and Cornwall that carried both the sets of initials, SR and GWR. At the other end of the scale, the title British Railways appeared again in 1931 at the Schoolboys' Exhibition, while towards the end of the decade the stands at the Toronto and New York World's Fair exhibitions were similarly run by the British railways as a whole, even if the LMS did exhibit the disguised 'Duchess of Hamilton' as part of the 'Coronation Scot' train at the latter. Such arrangements were entirely informal, but there were other joint activities which required legal approval. In 1933 the Great Western received ministerial approval for two agreements with the LNER and LMS, pooling the receipts for traffic conveyed by rail between certain places, which, from the public's point of view, permitted a wider interavailability of tickets. The importance attached to the agreements by the GWR was indicated by the fact that it was the first matter referred to in the *Great Western Railway Magazine* in May that year.

Having, with all the benefits of hindsight, set the economic scene during the 1930s, we will now be able to review the various specific developments that took place during the period in the numerous different departments of the Great Western.

Before that, however, this is the most appropriate place to record the absorption of another separate railway into the Western Group on 4 August 1930. This was the Corris, which was an 8½-mile narrow-gauge line in Central Wales, connecting with the GWR at Machynlleth. It was involved in a deal between the GWR and the Bristol Tramways & Carriage Company, the successors to the Imperial Tramway Company which had owned the Corris since 1878. The limited passenger services did not survive 1930 under GWR control, but the line continued to operate for freight until 1948. Two of the steam locomotives were subsequently sold to the Talyllyn Railway, and, as 'Sir Haydn' and 'Edward Thomas', played vital roles in the development of the first preserved railway in the world.

2
Motive Power and Rolling Stock

In spite of the difficult financial situation that faced the country throughout the 1930s, the Great Western continued to build considerable numbers of new locomotives during the period. It might thus appear that those in charge of the motive power department were not exerting their share of economy during the hard financial times. However, the steam locomotive, although simple and cheap to construct, required considerable maintenance. During the 1930s, for instance, the percentage of the total Great Western stock receiving works attention during the year varied between 50 and 69, having dropped from a post-World War I peak of 75 per cent in 1929. This level of works activity was related to the engine miles run during the year, but the swings in the numbers being overhauled were proportionally greater than the changes in the distances run during the year concerned. The annual repair bill for an average locomotive worked out at about 12 per cent of its initial cost, but such an overall figure would undoubtedly have hidden a large variation between different classes. In particular, as the LMS's detailed figures showed, the older and less-numerous locomotive classes would have been more expensive to maintain than those newly-constructed to the company's standard designs, particularly as the latter frequently had boilers that could be used on a number of different classes. So there could be a strong economic case for renewing the older locomotives on the company's strength, particularly if, at the same time, it permitted the total number to be decreased. This is what happened during the early part of the 1930s, as shown in Table 1. The 'golden year' of 1937 saw a reverse in the overall drop of 8 per cent since 1930 and the numbers thereafter climbed slightly, no doubt as a result of rearmament.

In the course of its policy of locomotive standardisation, which it had been following since the 1900s, the Great Western had already introduced its biggest and most powerful passenger classes, the Castles and Kings, by the end of the 1920s. Further examples of both these successful designs were constructed in the 1930s. The last batch of ten Kings entered service between May and July 1930, although a further single locomotive was constructed in 1936 as a replacement for No 6007 'King William III', badly damaged in the Shrivenham collision that year. Construction of more locomotives of the Castle class was resumed in 1932, after a gap of

Table 1 GREAT WESTERN
LOCOMOTIVE STOCK

Year	Average stock during year
1930	3884
1931	3865
1932	3802
1933	3756
1934	3710
1935	3609
1936	3591
1937	3604
1938	3637
1939	3638

Source: GWR General Statistics, October 1941 edition

five years, and by the outbreak of World War II a further eighty-five had entered service, a batch being built in every year except 1933. The mixed traffic 4–6–0 had also appeared with the conversion of 'Saint Martin' in 1924, and construction of the class proper began in earnest in 1928. Seventy were in service by the end of 1929, and construction continued throughout the 1930s. Each year except 1932 and 1934 saw the appearance of another batch, and even the outbreak of hostilities did not stop the construction of further locomotives of this class although, as dictated by the national policy, the building of the express passenger Castles halted for the duration.

The 1930s also saw the appearance of several new classes. Between 1936 and 1939 Swindon constructed eighty Granges, a further version of the mixed-traffic 4–6–0s. Although not appearing for twelve years after the conversion of the first Hall, the idea of a 4–6–0 with 5ft 8in diameter driving wheels had in fact been outlined by Churchward as far back as 1901. They were, in theory at least, renewals of some of the Churchward 2–6–0s which were built in batches from 1911 right through to 1932. During the

1920s it was found that some of them, operating in areas such as Cornwall, were suffering an unacceptable amount of wear to the flanges of the leading driving wheels, which markedly increased their maintenance costs. A number were accordingly modified by putting a large weight behind the front buffer-beam. This increased the loading on the pony truck, which in turn made it more effective in imparting side thrust to the frames on the curves, and so having the desired result of reducing the wear on the driving wheel flanges. Unfortunately this restricted the locomotives' route availability and in order to indicate this to 'the man on the line' they were accordingly renumbered in a separate 83XX series. The leading bogie on the Granges was an even better solution to the problem and several of the modified 2–6–0s were included among those withdrawn for conversion, athough only the wheels and motion of the earlier locomotives were actually reused. It was originally intended to renew all the 300-plus Moguls, but the programme was stopped by World War II.

The GWR had a system that indicated the classes of locomotive which were permitted to run on various different lines. These were classified by means of a series of colours which could be shown on maps. The Granges, like the modified 2–6–0s, were restricted to the 'Red' routes, and in order to provide a modern 4–6–0 capable of operating over the more lightly-built 'Blue' lines, the Manors were designed. Again, they were nominal renewals of the 2–6–0s, but five tons lighter. The first to appear in 1938 were used on the Newcastle-Swansea service which crossed the Cotswolds by the lightly-built secondary route between Banbury and Cheltenham. During World War II some were transferred to Oswestry and became the first 4–6–0s to work over the one-time Cambrian Railways' lines. Another duty, in their later years, was to

H. C. Casserley

2. The Scrap Yard at Swindon in October 1933 showing many of the locomotives replaced by more modern designs. The only one whose number is visible is no 162 which was an 0–6–2 tank from the Cardiff Railway. Originally numbered 27, it was built in 1887 and withdrawn for possible sale in July 1932.

pilot Kings and Castles on expresses over the South Devon banks between Newton Abbot and Plymouth, replacing the four-coupled Bull-dogs on this duty. This was a post-World War II continuation of a trend that was very marked in the 1930s when there was a wholesale switch from four-coupled to six-coupled locomotives for passenger traffic. Between 1930 and 1939 the Great Western's stock of 4–6–0s increased from 301 to 554 while the numbers of 4–4–0s declined from 250 to 93. One of the withdrawn 4–4–0s was 'City of Truro', the locomotive involved in the 1904 record run with the Ocean Mail Special from Plymouth to Bristol. Instead of being scrapped, it was restored and sent for exhibition at the LNER's railway museum at York, in due course becoming part of the National Collection after a brief return to main-line running.

In spite of the general move away from four-coupled designs, in 1936 Swindon combined parts from two separate classes of 4–4–0 rather than build new locomotives. The frames of twenty-nine of the Bulldogs were fitted with

3. Static testing. 'Shooting Star' running at the equivalent of 85 mph on the testing plant at Swindon in January 1932. This locomotive was converted to a Castle in 1925, and in 1936 was renumbered and renamed 100A1 'Lloyds' at a ceremony at Paddington station. The test plant was constructed in 1904 and its capacity was extended just before World War II to enable it to handle the latest locomotives at full output.

cabs from a similar number of Dukes, the last nine having new boilers. They became known as the Dukedogs although a start was made to name them after Earls. It was quickly decided that the peers concerned rated something more imposing than a hybrid renewal. The names applied to the first twelve were thus removed in

the summer of 1937, to reappear on the much more dignified Castle class. Other examples of renaming occurred in the 1930s when the last two Kings became 'King Edward VIII' and 'King George VI' in 1936 and 1937 respectively, to commemorate the country's new monarchs.

The Great Western's stock of 2–8–0s remained unchanged at 143 from 1931 to 1938, when construction of a modernised version of Churchward's heavy freight locomotives commenced. They had outside steam pipes and side-window cabs, being referred to as the 2884 Class. During the gap of twenty years since

4. Mobile Testing. 4–6–0 no 4930 'Hagley Hall' at
Swindon ready to carry out a test run. Behind the tender is
the dynamometer car, while a shelter has been fitted to the
front of the locomotive to protect the staff taking indicator
diagrams from the cylinders. Swindon played a large part in
the development of scientific testing of steam locomotives
in Britain.

H. C. Casserley Collection

the last of the earlier locomotives was built,
the Great Western had purchased a number of
the war-surplus ROD 2–8–0s of Great Central
design, the fifty best surviving in permanent
stock after 1931 and acquiring various Swindon
features before they were finally scrapped after
World War II. Certain of the tenders attached to
those locomotives that were withdrawn in the
late 1920s were in good enough condition to be
used with Great Western locomotives, in spite of
being of non-standard design.

The Great Western had introduced the 2–8–0
tank design before World War II, primarily for
use in the South Wales coalfield, and continued

to build batches of these new locomotives
throughout the 1920s. During the Great Depression there was little work for some of the
class. Certain of the locomotives never operated
in this form, and between 1934 and 1939 were
among the fifty or so that were converted to
2–8–2Ts. The extra carrying axle permitted the
construction of an enlarged bunker, which put
the coal capacity up from three to five tons and
enabled the locomotives to carry 2,500 gallons
of water compared with 1,800. In their new
guise they were capable of taking over the duties
of the older outside-framed Aberdare 2–6–0s
which were reaching the end of their economic
lives. Following the success of these conversions, a scheme was prepared for a massive
2–10–2T intended for the Ebbw Vale iron ore
traffic, but it was never built.

Much further down the scale, Collett produced two completely new designs in the 1930s.

H. C. Casserley

5. The first Grange under construction in Swindon Works. No 6800 was named 'Arlington Grange'. Initially the first three locomotives in the class were fitted with plain cast-iron chimneys, but later they were given the more imposing copper-capped variety like the rest of the class.

The first of these was the 2251 Class 0–6–0, intended as a replacement for the Dean goods locomotives with the same wheel arrangement, the youngest of which had been built in 1899, while veterans of the class were sixteen years older still. The new locomotives utilised the Swindon No 10 taper boiler which was first built in 1925 for fitting to some of the locomotives absorbed at the grouping. Although somewhat heavier than the locomotives they replaced, they had a wide sphere of activity on branches throughout the system, as well as handling lighter workings on the main lines. The locomotives they were designed to replace did not, however, entirely disappear from the scene. Some of those withdrawn just before World War II were reinstated and the class did not finally become extinct until 1957. Many saw overseas service in World War II, and some even finished their operational life in China under the auspices of the United Nations.

The smallest of Collett's locomotives were the 0–4–2 tanks built from 1932 onwards. They were designed as replacements for similar locomotives that dated back as far as 1868, and were being rapidly withdrawn at that period. Most of the class were fitted with equipment to work auto trains, and they could be found

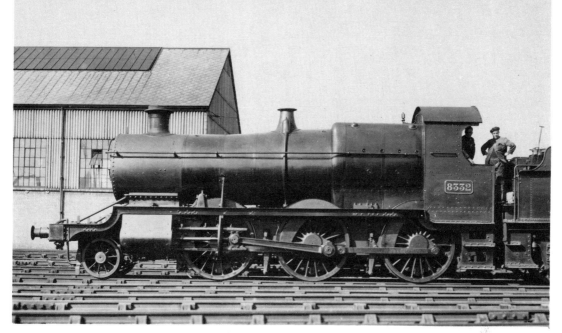

H. C. Casserley

6. One of the Churchward Moguls modified to run on lines where curvature was frequent. The heavy weight behind the front buffer beam can be seen. This reduced the wear on the flanges of the leading driving wheels. Built in 1917, no 5332 ran in modified form as no 8332 from 1928 to 1944, and was not scrapped until 1960.

pottering around the lightest of the branch lines throughout the system. Some of them took over from the steam rail motors, the last of which was withdrawn in 1935, and could even have found themselves working auto cars converted from the self-propelled steam units. For the heavier push-pull operations a new design of 0–6–0 pannier tank had appeared in 1931 after trials of a prototype, converted from a locomotive constructed at the turn of the century. The larger standard panniers of the 57XX Class continued to be built throughout the 1930s, considerable quantities of them being purchased from outside firms rather than constructed at Swindon.

There was, however, an even more significant motive-power development in the 1930s, when the Great Western introduced its first stream-lined diesel railcar in late 1933. It was initially referred to as an Experimental Stream-lined Heavy Oil Rail Car and considerable changes took place as the successive designs were developed. The first unit had a single diesel motor, and was unique in this respect, all the others having a pair, one driving each bogie. Fluid flywheels and pre-selective epicyclic gear boxes were fitted to transmit the power to the axles, although on some cars one engine could only be brought into use after the speed had reached the point where it could drive the other bogie by means of a simple clutch. This avoided the need for a second gear box. A batch of twenty second-generation cars was authorised in 1938 although they did not actually appear until the war years. These had considerably more traditional railway features, and the underframes with buffers and draw-gear were actually constructed at Swindon. Some were capable of being coupled together, the electro-magnetic controls enabling the driver to operate all the

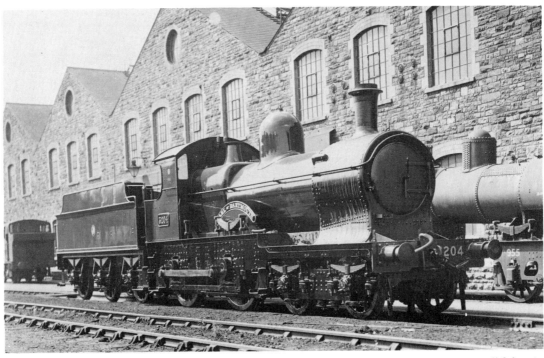

7. One of the Dukedogs that resulted from combining the boilers and cabs off the Duke class 4–4–0s with the frames from some of the Bulldog class. They were an excellent example of the Great Western's economic approach to problems. No 3204, seen here at Swindon in August 1936, was at first named 'Earl of Dartmouth' but, as with the early members of the class that were similarly adorned, the name was later transferred to a Castle 4–6–0.

motors simultaneously. This was an important step forward, and the vast majority of the large British Railways fleet of diesel-railcars built since World War II have used exactly the same form of transmission with full multiple-unit capability.

The first of the railcars was introduced on suburban services between Paddington and Slough, but the next batch of three cars was built for express passenger services and contained a small buffet. They were introduced on a new express service between Cardiff and Birmingham, a supplement of 2s 6d (12½p) being charged. The significance of these units is acknowledged by the inclusion of no 4 in the National Collection. By the summer of 1935, when there were seven cars in service, they were being rostered for a total daily mileage of 1,193. Assuming one of the fleet was spare, this meant each was averaging nearly 200 miles daily. Other railcars were designed for use on branch lines, and later examples were capable of hauling a trailer coach or vacuum-fitted vans. Two of the thirty-eight cars built altogether were for express parcels traffic. While the Great Western pioneered the use of multiple-unit diesel railcars, it did not move forward as fast as the LMS did with the development of the diesel-electric shunter. After purchasing a Fowler diesel-

8. One of the 2–8–0 tanks that were converted to the 2–8–2 wheel arrangement between 1934 and 1939 when replacements were required for the aging Aberdare 2–6–0 tender locomotives. No 7205 was photographed at Swindon in August 1936.

H. C. Casserley

mechanical shunter to use at Swindon in 1933, they obtained a solitary 0–6–0 diesel-electric from Hawthorn Leslie three years later, which was used in the new yard at Acton up to World War II.

The diesel railcars were not the only example of streamlining adopted by the Great Western. In the same way as the epithet 'jet' has been applied over the last decade or so to indicate anything that was supposed to be right up to date, the adjective 'streamlined' was used in the 1930s to emphasise the latest developments in all forms of transport. In March 1935, Swindon streamlined a King and a Castle. There were differences between the two classes, but the most

obvious features involved fitting a bullet-nose to the smokebox, farings behind the chimney and safety-valve bonnet, continuous splashers and a V-shaped cab front. The results were not aesthetically very pleasing, but nevertheless caused a lot of interest at the time, particularly as the modifications enabled the GWR to beat the LNER with the first streamlined locomotive, since the first of Gresley's A4s did not appear until much later that year. The various GWR fitments caused some operating difficulties, however, and they disappeared progressively over the years, although 'King Henry VII' retained its wedge-shaped cab to the end.

In a book of this length it is not possible to chronicle all the Great Western motive power developments that took place during a single decade. Many books have been written on this

H. C. Casserley

9. An example of Collett's 2251 class 0–6–0s for branch lines which were designed as replacements for the Dean Goods locomotives of the same wheel arrangement. No 2259 stands at Reading in August 1930.

subject, and those wanting the full detail should study the excellent and authoritative series produced by the Railway Correspondence & Travel Society. It is worth, however, making reference to one particular small change that took place on Great Western locomotives during the 1930s, as it indicates the lengths to which that railway was prepared to go in the cause of safety. In the October 1931 issue of the *Great Western Railway Magazine* there is a photograph showing how a fireman on a moving locomotive caught the pricker on an over-bridge and was thrown off the footplate to his death. It is always a tricky operation turning a pricker end-for-end on a steam locomotive. This has to be done twice every time it is used, as it has to be stowed on the tender with the sharp end to the rear. After use it is invariably hot, and keeping it within the confines of the cab and loading gauge is virtually impossible. Following the accident referred to,

the Great Western's solution was to provide the larger locomotives with a sheet-metal compartment along the left-hand side of the foot-framing beside the firebox, so the fire-irons could be stowed there rather than on the tender, which avoided having to turn them round. In the case of the Halls, the change-over started with 'Bingley Hall', the first of the class to be built after the incident in 1931.

Turning now to the rolling stock side, there were a number of significant steps forward during the 1930s with passenger carriages. Great Western coaching stock was always a lot more varied than the locomotives, as contemporary photographs of their trains show only too clearly. It was usually only the prestige trains that had a complete rake of matching stock, and space does not permit even a passing reference to many of the variants produced during this particular decade. Michael Harris, in his authoritative book on Great Western coaches, sums up the first half of the 1930s when he says that the ordinary vehicles completed in the period 1933–

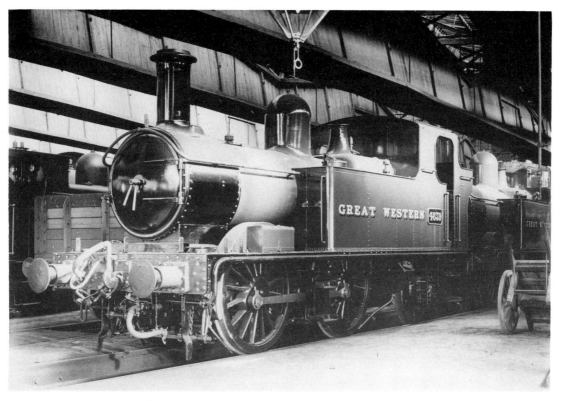

10. Two of the new 0–4–2 tanks built from 1932 onwards. No 4839 was constructed in 1934. After World War II the class were renumbered in the 14XX series to enable their original numbers to be used for those standard 2–8–0 freight locomotives that were converted for oil burning.

1936 were 'probably the most undistinguished of GWR coaches'.

There were, however, two significant design features that began to appear during the late 1930s which are still familiar to us today. The first of these features came into extensive use on GWR stock in the second half of the 1930s, and was the elimination of the external door to each compartment on corridor stock, which markedly improved the whole ambience of long-distance train travel, as it simultaneously removed the hassle caused by passengers joining

and alighting having to push past those already sitting down, and also gave a far better view through the large single 'picture' window. Nowadays we are used to this layout, all corridor compartment stock built to the BR standard design having this feature, but as far as the GWR is concerned it first appeared on the 'Centenary' stock of 1935. These vehicles were introduced for the newly-styled 'Cornish Riviera Limited' for the summer of 1935 as part of the celebrations for the centenary of the passing of the railway's first Act of Parliament. The external design closely followed the pattern set by the 'Super Saloons' and the 1929 'Riviera' restaurant cars, with an overall width of 9ft 7in, the recessed end doors mounted at an angle to the

British Rail Western Region

11. The Great Western used considerable numbers of
2–6–2 tanks on branch lines and suburban services. The
basic design went back to 1903, but in the late 1930s ten of
the earlier locomotives from the 51XX series were
renewed as nos 8100–09. In the photograph no 8103 is
seen at Swindon. The pick-up shoe for the Automatic Train
Control can be seen under the front buffer beam.

body giving the vehicles a characteristic appearance. The large windows could initially be
dropped as a whole, but difficulties were caused
by the shape of the bodyside and they were later
fixed with sliding ventilators at the tops, of the
same general type we know today.

Following the appearance of these coaches
which, until the war, were only used on the

'Riviera', the same compartment arrangements
were generally adopted for all new corridor
stock. The large windows in the corridor side
were also arranged to coincide as much as
possible with the position of the compartments
to improve the view for the passengers. There
were variations on the general theme over the
following few years, with one compartment
acquiring an external door, while four doors
were adopted on the corridor side in the interests
of more rapid boarding and alighting at stations.
These 'Sunshine' coaches were very popular
with passengers, and it is amusing to recall that
the introduction of the same feature on the

12. The start of the streamline era on the GWR. A steam locomotive passes the pioneer streamlined railcar no 1 between Paddington and Reading. This vehicle was provided with suitably-labelled doors on both sides of each cab for the driver.

'Dreadnoughts' in the mid-1900s caused considerable criticism, although, to be fair, the elimination of the external compartment doors was not then accompanied by the installation of large windows. The ordinary 'Sunshine' stock was built to a width of 9ft to give it a wider route availability over the Great Western, but the 1938 designs were an inch narrower still. This permitted them to work on through trains over the LMS and LNER, and they were distinguished by a yellow disc on the ends, near the customary raised figures giving the vehicles' weights.

The second new feature of note with the Great Western stock in the mid-1930s was the construction of some attractively-styled centre-corridor excursion trains, with tables between each set of seats. This layout, now more usually referred to as 'open', has become increasingly popular in the last decade or so, to such an extent that all the day-time Mk III vehicles built by BR have such an arrangement. Similar trains of excursion stock had been built by the other railways, but when the Swindon version appeared in 1935 the interior was far more attractively styled than any of its rivals. Light wooden finishes were extensively used, with darker edging around the stepped angular doorways and mirrors, while unusual cubic lamp shades were provided in place of the more-or-less universal bare bulb. The well-upholstered low-backed seats gave passengers an immediate impression of comfort, in marked contrast to the LNER Tourist coach equivalent.

Although many minor variations in livery took place during the 1930s, 1934 saw the introduction of one very obvious small change.

25

13. Streamlined railcars nos 10–12 entered service in January 1936. This photograph shows all three being delivered from the Southall Works of the Associated Equipment Company. The bodies of these cars were built by the Gloucester Railway Carriage & Wagon Co, and the separate doors for the driver have disappeared.

No longer did the locomotives and carriages carry the company's 'coat of arms', comprising those of the cities of London and Bristol placed side by side. Instead the GWR monogram was used, formed in spidery angular letters, and surrounded by an even thinner circular line. This became more or less universal throughout the company, but the spindliness and lack of colour did nothing for the corporate image. There was universal acclaim when the 'coat of arms' was readopted after the austerity of World War II.

Another obvious change in coach livery was the decision in 1933 to eliminate the use of the word 'Third' on the exterior.

Special mention must be made of one particular class of eight vehicles, the 'Super Saloons' built in 1931. As we saw in Volume I, the Great Western did considerable business with the prestigious trans-Atlantic liners which called at Plymouth. Pullman cars were used on the Ocean Liner specials for a short period, starting in 1929, but the Great Western decided to build a set of its own coaches, every bit as luxurious as the Pullmans. The company was exceptionally proud of the vehicles that resulted, and they even rated a colour supplement to the *Great Western Railway Magazine* in January 1932. The overall layout was similar to the first-class Pullmans, with open saloons and coupés, but full advantage was taken of the GWR loading gauge. An overall width of 9ft 7in was adopted, with angled and recessed end doors. Like first-class Pullmans, the 'Super Saloons' were named, using those of the Royal Family, and they were operated extensively in special trains of all sorts. One was provided for the Duke and Duchess of Kent's honeymoon in November 1934. In Ocean Liner service they commanded a 10s (50p) supplement over and above first-class fare, which should be compared with the corresponding first-class charge of only 5s (25p) for the 'Silver Jubilee' on the much longer Newcastle-King's Cross journey. Nevertheless, in 1932 over 2,300 passengers used them on the Ocean Liner specials.

We must now turn our attention to the other end of the scale to consider the Great Western's freight rolling stock, which, it must be remembered, provided more of the company's revenue than did the passengers. The 1930s were, however, not a period when there was any great leap forward in the design of vans or wagons generally, the vast majority of the vehicles being

14. The streamlined Castle 4–6–0 no 5005 'Manorbier Castle', seen here at Temple Meads station in Bristol in 1935.

of simple design, devoid of continuous brakes, and rugged enough to withstand being trundled around the country in the course of their very small annual usage, made at low speed throughout. During the 1930s the GWR's freight workings never averaged as much as ten miles per train hour. Even so they were consistently better than those on the LMS and LNER, although in some years the Southern's trains averaged a few hundred yards per hour more than the Great Western's. Even when in 1933 the GWR was trying to interest collieries in leasing a new batch of twenty-ton steel coal wagons, the carefully annotated financial calculations assumed only one journey a fortnight. These particular vehicles were a batch of 5,000 ordered in 1933 with Government financial assistance under the 1929 Act at a total cost of £1.1 million.

Photo Source Fox

15. The interior of one of the GWR Super Saloons used for Ocean Liner Specials and on other prestigious occasions. In this photograph, taken in November 1934, staff at Swindon make sure the interior is fully up to the standard required for the honeymoon train conveying the Duke and Duchess of Kent.

The simplicity of the average coal wagon between the World Wars is also worth noting. Even the capital cost of the new-fangled, all-steel forty-tonners being pioneered by the GWR worked out at only £220 each, but the maintenance cost was very low too. The library at the National Railway Museum has a little booklet, produced by the Wagon Repairs Association in late 1923, quoting the rates they would charge for overhaul contracts. At that time, for a seven-year contract on a new eight- or ten-ton wagon built to the 'new specification', they were prepared to quote a figure of only £2 7s 3d (£2.36) per year. Between 1923 and 1930 the retail price index dropped by 7 per cent. The fall in wholesale prices was even more dramatic, being down by 17 per cent at the beginning of 1930, and reaching a low in 1933 that represented a total fall of 36 per cent. By inference, therefore, the repair costs in the 1930s were unlikely to have been much higher than those quoted for 1923. The figures in the 1923 tables

28

British Rail Western Region

16. The 6-wheeled van no 2802 left one in no doubt what it was intended to carry. The photograph was taken in December 1936.

17. A line of Goods Fruit Vans at Weymouth Quay in May 1938, with the doors opened to show how the boxes of Guernsey produce were packed inside.

British Rail Western Region

were inclusive of haulage to the repair depots, but excluded the cost of replacing any wheels. General painting was carried out only every three years or so, with extra charges for any special lettering. Older wagons clearly required more attention but even so the annual cost for a seven-year contract for eight-year-old wagons was less than the five-guinea (£5.25) price of a Hornby Gauge O 'Princess Elizabeth' locomotive and tender in 1937. (Nowadays even the model catalogue would raise more than that in the second-hand railway book market, such have been the effects of inflation and the widespread development of the collecting hobby.) It is against figures like these that one must judge the slow development of railway freight wagons in the 1930s.

As we have already seen, the Great Western in the 1920s realised that there were considerable advantages from the use of the twenty-ton coal wagon, and was finding new ways of widening their adoption. The principle was extended to other freight vehicles too, a new high-capacity design for steel being introduced experimentally in South Wales early in 1931, while one of the railway's customers was at the same time using twenty-ton limestone wagons discharged by tippler. Later the same year the Great Western produced its 'Mink G' twenty-ton high-capacity vans. With a wheelbase of just under twenty feet, they were vacuum braked and fitted with Instanter couplings. Although they represented a general step forward, the company had already a handful of thirty-ton vans in use. Another variant was the 'Grano' of 1935, a twenty-ton steel hopper wagon for grain.

In contrast to these general-purpose freight vehicles, there were quite a lot of developments with the more specialised types. More containers of various sorts were introduced, some specially designed for bicycles, while others for perishable traffic were equipped for cooling by

18. One of the Great Western's shock-absorbing vans. Like the fruit vans in the previous illustration, this vehicle carries a prominent notice requiring it to be returned to the GWR when emptied, as it was not part of the common user 'pool'.

'Drikold', the solid carbon dioxide refrigerant developed by ICI at Billingham, which itself was to be distributed extensively throughout the country in their own highly-insulated special containers. Demountable milk tanks were also introduced to supplement the earlier variety. The Great Western's first shock-absorbing van was built for trials in 1938 following the LMS's lead, and the same year saw the construction of the first batch of 200 new 'Fruits A', which were twelve-ton ventilated vans with vacuum brakes and screw couplings suitable for seasonal traffics such as broccoli, plums or tomatoes. By 1939 the fall-off in animals being moved by rail resulted in some 300 surplus cattle vans also being modified for fruit traffic, while a further fifty were adapted as 'ale wagons'. Another well-known type of vehicle to make its appearance in 1936 was the insulated six-wheel van for Palethorpes 'Royal Cambridge' sausages, suit-

19. One of the GWR Camp Coaches. This is no 9980 of clerestory design.

H. C. Casserley Collection

ably decorated on its sides and capable of operating in passenger trains. Throughout the 1930s the Great Western's freight vehicle stock fluctuated closely around the figure of 80,000, but there were in addition all the private-owner wagons also in use. Common-user arrangements applied between the main-line companies for most general-purpose vehicles, the standards of construction being laid down by the Railway Clearing House, which also monitored the use each company made of the 'pool', and raised charges accordingly.

Easter 1934 marked the start of the Great Western's Camping Coaches, sited at selected stations in the West of England and Wales, a facility that was to become very well-known over the next quarter-century and which, in modified form, is still with us. The success of the first season's trials resulted in an extension of the idea, and in the light of experience an internal connection was provided between the living and sleeping compartments, which must have added considerably to their appeal. Those booking them for holidays were expected to travel by train, and the new Holiday Season Tickets were also available to enable journeys to be made in the same area. Nowadays such tickets are called 'Rovers', having in the interim been advertised under the brand-name of 'Runabouts'. The railways also used to sell off their old coach bodies for 'grounding' as holiday chalets, and there was a particularly notable instance of this in 1935. A saloon which had once been part of Queen Victoria's Royal Train was sold and moved to Aberporth on Cardigan Bay. The event rated an account in the *Great Western Railway Magazine*, but few would have expected the vehicle to be recovered nearly half a century later to become part of the 'Royalty & Railways' exhibition at Windsor.

3
New Ways and Works

Throughout the 1930s the Great Western was very busily engaged on numerous large-scale improvements to its main lines. A very high proportion of the investment was guaranteed by the Government in one way or another, starting with the Development (Load Guarantees and Grants) Act of 1929. Over the decade the company invested a further £13.3 million, the figures for their total capital expenditure at two-yearly intervals being as follows:

Table 2 TOTAL GWR CAPITAL EXPENDED

	(£ million)
1929	174.1
1931	179.4
1933	182.5
1935	184.1
1937	185.4
1939	187.4

Source: GWR Annual Reports

Compared with the other main-line companies, the Great Western spent more on capital account than either the LMS or LNER, and was only eclipsed by the Southern with its extensive dock development and electrification schemes.

It will be seen that the highest rate of expenditure was in the earlier years, and at the beginning of 1931 the company reported that thirty-four different schemes had been authorised. At that time only two had been completed; the doubling of the Scorrier-Redruth and the Bugle-Goonbarrow Junction sections in Cornwall. The former marked the provision of double track for the whole distance from Paddington to Penzance, with the sole exception of Saltash Bridge, but during the next few years the railway was to quadruple considerable lengths of this, their prime route for the rapidly-growing holiday traffic. The Act covered a wide variety of schemes and before the end of that year the company was able to report the completion of the eighteen following works:

Banbury – New marshalling yard.
Severn Tunnel Junction – Enlargement of marshalling yard.
Scorrier to Redruth – Doubling of line.
Rogerstone – Enlargement of marshalling yard.
Bugle to Goonbarrow Junction – Doubling of line.
Paignton – New goods depot and reconstruction of passenger station.
Wolverhampton – Reconstruction of goods depot.
Radyr – Provision of new engine shed.

Treherbert – New engine shed, improved coaling and watering facilities.

Cardiff (Cathays) – New carriage shop.

Swindon – Re-arrangement of locomotive shops.

Duffryn Yard – Improvement of coaling facilities.

Pantyffynnon – New engine shed.

Extension of automatic train control.

Hockley – Extension of warehouse.

Swansea (High Street) – New warehouse.

Lye – Provision of additional mileage sidings and improved goods shed facilities.

Small Heath – Provision of a new goods warehouse.

A total of forty different schemes had been approved by the Government, but two proposals for dock improvements in South Wales had been abandoned by the end of 1931. Clearly the Government's financial incentive of interest grants at up to 5 per cent for periods of between five and fifteen years was not enough to compensate for the dramatic economic turn-down in that area, as we shall see in Chapter 5.

The provisions of the Development (Loan Guarantees and Grants) Act of 1929 were followed in 1935 by more special financial arrangements to assist the railway companies. They were modelled on the London Passenger Transport (Agreement) Act of that year, which will be discussed separately later. Under the Railways (Agreement) Act, the Railway Finance Corporation Ltd was formed by the Treasury, and the main-line companies were able to borrow the capital required for approved new schemes from the corporation at preferential rates of interest. By the end of 1935, therefore, the GWR was able to announce a whole series of new improvement schemes involving the planned expenditure of £5½ million over the next five years. Because of the overwhelming emphasis

the Great Western placed on the up-grading of the West of England main line during the 1930s, the most effective way of conveying an impression of all these developments is on a geographical rather than chronological basis.

At Paddington, the hub of the company's activities in London, the station and its various facilities were very extensively rebuilt in the period 1932–34. This followed a comprehensive report produced in September 1928 by the Chief Engineer entitled 'The Future of Paddington Station'. Not all the original suggestions were however adopted, such as the proposal for a reinforced concrete roof to the train shed or the idea of putting a 300-feet high clock tower on top of the offices. When it came to practicalities, the platforms themselves were extended, and the whole of the permanent-way layout was remodelled over the first three-quarters of a mile, colour-light signalling and power-operated points being provided. The former Bishop's Road station on the up side was replaced by the four new Paddington suburban platforms, serving the London Transport trains as well as the Great Western's. A new parcels depot was constructed on the down side beyond the end of no 1 platform, stretching out beneath Westbourne Bridge. On the other side of the tracks, a slice had to be cut off the wall of the goods depot to accommodate the sweep of the suburban tracks, giving the unusual end profile to the building that remains to this day. Extensive rebuilding took place at the Lawn end of the station, with two new office blocks, one at each side, linked by a most unusual cross-corridor at first-floor level along the back of the hotel. The whole operation was immense and involved great engineering ingenuity to plan and execute. The year 1934 also saw work start on the enlarged carriage sidings and other facilities at Old Oak Common, which was to continue throughout the 1930s.

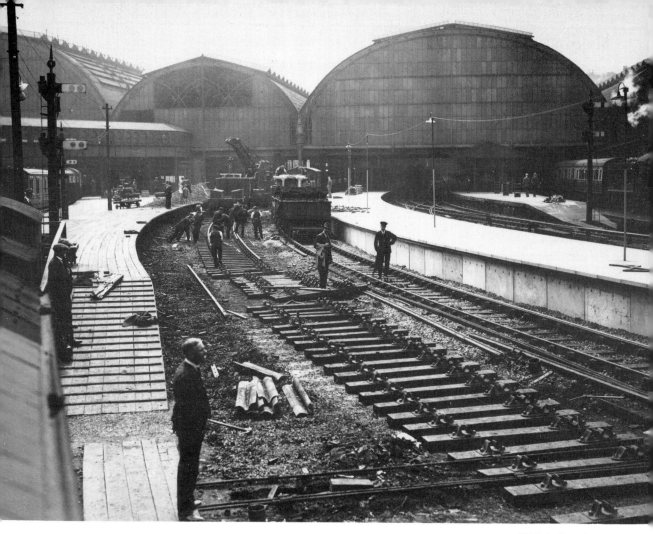

20. A view of the reconstruction work at Paddington. The photograph was taken on 21 June 1931 during an engineering occupation that lasted from 1 am to 4 pm and involved unloading considerable quantities of material for the lengthening of No 8 platform on the left.

Moving westwards, the next major improvements on the West of England line were the Westbury and Frome cut-offs, opened in 1932. When the Great Western introduced its new route to the west in 1906, there had been a great saving in distance, but all expresses had to thread the tortuous curves and junctions at these two

towns. The 1932 cut-offs, although only marginally shorter, eliminated the slowings necessary for non-stop trains, a factor in timetable planning which had become even more significant as loads had increased. To mark the change, the timetables started referring to non-stop trains, like the 'Riviera', as running 'Via Castle Cary' instead of 'Via Westbury'.

The year 1932 also saw the quadrupling of some eight miles of line through Taunton, between Cogload Junction and Norton Fitz-

21. The interior of the new Paddington departure signal box. The use of a track circuit diagram is combined with a power frame.

BBC Hulton Picture Library

warren, which was coupled with extensive alterations to the county town's station itself. Cogload is the meeting point of the Great Western's two routes to the west, and the flat junction there was a potential cause of delay at peak periods with trains on the Castle Cary line conflicting with the increased traffic from the Midlands via Bristol. To overcome this a new fly-over junction was built, the extreme skew of the tracks passing underneath the down Bristol line, resulting in the use of a pair of very asymmetrical main girders. As part of the alterations the signal box was moved bodily to its new position in four easy stages, using a pair of steam cranes. (Elsewhere it was not unknown for similar movements of complete boxes to be made by manpower, after preliminary jacking to make the box mobile.) The Taunton quadrupling continued westwards to Norton Fitzwarren, the junction for the Barnstaple and Minehead branches. Improvements were subsequently made to both these lines, with four new crossing loops being provided on the latter while the former was doubled as far as Milverton, the first station. Furthermore, both lines were in time equipped with tablet changing-equipment to enable non-stop trains to take the loops at higher speeds than was possible with manual exchange of the vital single-line tablets.

Further west again, a number of intermediate stations on the main line were provided with platform loops, which enabled expresses to overtake stopping trains. Wellington, Sampford Peverell, Tiverton Junction, Cullumpton, Stoke

35

22. Wantage Road Station in April 1934 showing the new signal box and four-track layout, which involved the extension of the overbridge at the near end of the platforms. The bus in line with the station building belonged to the City of Oxford Motor Services, one of the GWR's associated road companies.

Canon and Exminster all came in for this treatment. In 1938 work was put in hand to reconstruct the station buildings at Exeter St David's, but the war prevented the proposed alterations being made to the platforms and track layout. At Plymouth North Road an extensive remodelling scheme was also undertaken in the same period. The first new platform came into service in 1938 but the completion was again overtaken by World War II when the station, like so much of the city, was badly hit during the air raids.

Reference has already been made to the completion of the doubling of the main line in Cornwall, but other facilities were needed in that county to deal with the growing traffic. Newquay became a major holiday resort, attracting enormous quantities of new railway business, and extensive alterations were required to handle them. The branch from Par could take 4–6–0 passenger locomotives, and to permit these to be turned easily at Newquay, improvements were made to the triangle at Tolcarne, just outside the station. Then in 1938 the imposing Trenance Viaduct, just clear of the end of the station platforms, was rebuilt. All nine of the original plate-girder spans were simultaneously moved six feet sideways across the tops of the extended granite piers, and new half-arches built alongside. After these had been completed, a new line was laid in, the plate

23. Rebuilding work in progress on the main up platform at Temple Meads, Bristol, in October 1934.

British Rail Western Region

girders demolished and the arches completed to full width for the second track. Today's average train on the Newquay branch is a three-car diesel multiple-unit, which looks lost in the main platform there, the only one normally used. It is however very interesting to see how this has been successively extended, the different forms of construction indicating the changes that took place over the years to handle longer and longer trains of holiday-makers.

Penzance, at the western end of the GWR's line, was also enlarged. The original single-line viaduct with its fifty-one wooden spans at the approach to the terminus had disappeared in 1920, but the station still boasted only a pair of short platforms. In 1938 work began on the provision of four longer ones, which involved the construction of a new sea wall made from granite. Truro, too, came in for its share of improvements during the same period, while the last of Brunel's timber viaducts in the West of England was replaced in 1935. This was at Collegewood, and was the longest of the eight replaced on the Falmouth Branch.

The work necessary to handle the increased holiday traffic in the west of England was not confined to civil engineering, as corresponding improvements had to be made to the signalling systems. Not only was it vital to provide new boxes to control the additional four-track sections, but intermediate boxes were con-

37

structed in various locations to increase the number of block sections available when trains were running at close head-ways.

However, the two most ambitious plans for improving the West of England services included in the schemes approved under the 1935 Act were never to be completed. These would have involved the construction of two completely new lines, the first, 8½ miles long, bypassing the coastal section through Dawlish and Teignmouth. The second would have comprised a new route linking St Germans with Looe, where a new hotel was planned. Both involved some very interesting engineering features, and their differing purposes provide a further insight into current Great Western thinking.

The sea wall protecting the main line at the foot of the red sandstone cliffs of Devon from Dawlish Warren to Teignmouth was a perennial problem to the civil engineers, with periodic wash-outs by the sea during storms. Rain or frost could dislodge sections of the cliff, and the speed of trains was also restricted to prevent similar trouble from excessive vibrations. It might thus be thought that the new line was intended to provide a more easily maintained alternative, but that would have resulted in two major Devon resorts having far more inconvenient stations some way inland on the diversion. The real purpose of the line, however, was to provide *additional* capacity, giving, in effect, an eight-mile section of quadruple main line. At peak times, too, trains would be able to call at Dawlish and Teignmouth without causing delays to other traffic when the services were running block-to-block. For those who know the South Devon topography, the 'new by-pass railway' would obviously have been difficult to construct. The main engineering feature was a tunnel, 1½ miles long, under Haldon Down, but there were three other shorter ones. Had the line been built, the alternating tunnels and valley crossings would have been somewhat reminiscent of twentieth-century Japanese railway construction, which has been carried to its extreme on parts of the Shinkansen with its rapid succession of tunnels and valleys. The Devon line would have included 'ramps' inclined at 1 in 150 at each end. The climbs of two to three miles would have been somewhat of an obstacle to a heavy express, even one hauled by a King, particularly as there would have been limited opportunity to get a run at them from either end. Although surveyed in detail, the line was never built, and we can fortunately still enjoy the incomparable views of the South Devon coast from the windows of the InterCity 125s.

For today's passengers on the main line through Cornwall, there are fleeting views of the Looe line from viaducts either side of Liskeard. Before the bypass road was built round the latter town, the full route of the branch line could be seen as it follows its tight horseshoe route up the valley at right-angles to the main line, climbing all the way to reach the station. West of Liskeard, the main line trains cross Moorswater Viaduct, threaded below by the extension of the line beyond Coombe Junction, where all trains must reverse during their journeys between Looe and Liskeard. The origins of these unusual arrangements go back to the independent Looe & Liskeard and Liskeard & Caradon Railways, not to mention the Liskeard & Looe Union Canal, but space does not permit us to dwell on the fascinating history of these companies. In the 1930s, however, the Great Western had the task of running a service to what was becoming a very popular holiday resort. Through trains were a virtual impossibility, with the Liskeard junction facing the wrong way towards Penzance, while the need to run-round at Coombe Junction posed other difficulties. In these days of diesel railcars the

24. The new locomotive shed at Laira, Plymouth, in May 1934. One of the branch-line 2–6–2 tanks, no 4591 is in the foreground, with a Castle beyond.

British Rail Western Region

operations at the latter point present few problems, but at times in the steam era branch trains were booked to *cross* in the loop there, with its single platform, which necessitated a considerable number of to and fro movements for the locomotives and stock.

The Great Western's 1936 proposal was to do away with that particular line for passengers and construct a totally new one running to a separate terminal station from a junction on the main line at St Germans. Again the topography necessitated a succession of Shinkansen-like tunnels and viaducts. Seaton Tunnel, the biggest of the three, was to have been 2,288 yards long, while Keveral Viaduct, carrying the line 144 feet above the river, would have had a length of 343 yards. It was a bold scheme, with an intermediate station at Downderry and a halt at Mildendreath. It was the intention to work a through service from Plymouth over the seven-mile branch using streamlined diesel railcars with an overall schedule of thirty-five minutes for a journey of about sixteen miles. Although that does not sound very quick, even by the standards of the 1930s, it would have been half-an-hour better than the existing services. Bearing in mind the difficulties and delays of the ferry crossings of the Tamar at Saltash and Tor Point, the new line would undoubtedly have stimulated considerable commuter traffic into Plymouth. (There was already an 08.00 train from St Germans to Millbay in the 1930s, while in the 1983–84 BR timetable the 06.28 HST from Penzance still fits in stops at St Germans and Saltash to get passengers to Plymouth at 08.22.) Furthermore the new line could easily have been the ultimate destination of through expresses from Paddington, the Midlands and the North, which would have done wonders for the tourist development of that particular section of the Cornish coast. The Great Western was poised to take advantage of this with a new hotel of its

25. The last of Brunel's timber viaducts were replaced in the 1930s. This final one was at Collegewood on the Falmouth branch, and the photograph shows the replacement being built alongside the original in May 1934.

own, complete with golf course, for which there was a capital contingency in the 1938 accounts. However, although work on the approach road began, together with preliminary operations to construct the line itself, World War II prevented the proposal becoming a reality, and the dream of the south-coast equivalent of the Tregenna Castle Hotel faded from the minds of the Great Western's corporate planners. The original branch to Looe has survived Beeching and Serpell, and one can only speculate on the train service that might have been running on the new line today had it been built. Through HST workings on summer Saturdays from Manchester or Newcastle are only some of the possibilities that come to mind.

Although the West of England route clearly received a lot of attention during the 1930s, extensive improvements were also taking place elsewhere. Didcot was extensively remodelled, and three of the stations between there and Swindon were provided with platform loops giving four tracks through them. There were extensive improvements, too, in the Bristol area. Temple Meads station was enlarged to cover more than twice its previous area, while the length of the longest platform was increased from 920 to 1,340 feet. The original broad gauge terminal platforms and the striking facade of the station buildings were retained. In order to improve train working, additional running lines were provided so that there were four or more tracks all the way from Filton Junction, in the north, through Temple Meads itself, to Portishead Junction in the west, a distance of 6½ miles. This was the last scheme to be carried out under the 1929 Act and it was completed in 1935.

26. In April 1935 the new Collegewood Viaduct is in use, but the piers of Brunel's original structure continue to stand alongside, as is still the case with many of his viaducts in Devon and Cornwall, fifty years later.

British Rail Western Region

Another quadrupling scheme covered the nine miles from Olton to Lapworth through the commuter area south of Birmingham. To test the new underline bridges on this stretch, four of the Kings, coupled in pairs, were run over them one Sunday morning, at speeds of up to 60 mph, both pairs of locomotives being kept exactly abreast as they crossed each structure. Another major station reconstruction undertaken by the GWR in the late 1930s was at Leamington Spa.

Wales was not left out of the improvements. The reconstruction of Newport (High Street) was completed in 1930 after work had gone on for seven years, and in 1934 the Minister of Transport was able to open the new GWR station at Cardiff. Not only were the passenger facilities at the General station completely renewed, but extensive improvements were made to other railway installations in the vicinity. A new parcels depot was built and four tracks provided through the station for a distance of

1¾ miles. Canton Yard was completely remodelled, with improvements in the facilities for servicing passenger carriages and locomotives, while colour-light signalling was provided throughout the area. To serve the football ground, Ninian Park halt was enlarged. Further west, the improvements at Swansea (High Street), which had also begun in 1923, were completed. The first two full-length platforms had been finished in 1931, which enabled main-line trains to serve Swansea itself, instead of having to call at Landore.

Throughout the GWR system numerous new halts were constructed in the early 1930s, a particularly notable example being the one at The Hawthorns for the West Bromwich Albion football ground, which was actually opened, with due ceremony involving two Mayors, *on Christmas Day 1932*. This was one of a score of new halts brought into operation in 1932, compared with about fifteen in each of the preceding and following years, which gives some indication of the scale of these activities.

41

27. At Penzance it was necessary to build a new sea wall before the station could be enlarged. This photograph, looking towards the buffer stops, was taken in July 1938 and gives a good idea of the scale of the operations. A Hall stands in the station at the head of an up train. Many of the signals are out of use. Western National buses can be glimpsed in line with the gas-holder, typical of the convenient road–rail interchanges there were in Cornwall.

British Rail Western Region

Mention was made earlier of the financial arrangements made available by the London Passenger Transport (Agreement) Act of 1935. The Great Western was involved in this because it was used to fund the extensions of the Central Line. East of Liverpool Street, the tube trains were to be extended over a new section of line. This enabled them to reach the LNER branch to Ongar, which was to be converted for electric traction. The corresponding western extension was somewhat simpler and necessitated the widening of the GWR's main line to Birmingham from North Acton out to Ruislip. As a

journey along the line today shows, it actually involved far more than simple earth-moving operations and the laying of track equipment for third-rail electric trains. Although the actual operation of the new line and ownership of the stock was nothing to do with the GWR, it also built the tube rollingstock depot at Ruislip. For the work the GWR was able to borrow up to £2 million from the London Electric Transport Finance Corporation Ltd. The interest payments on this were funded from the receipts of the London Transport Pool. As the Great Western's share of these receipts was only slightly over one per cent, Paddington must have viewed the whole deal highly favourably. Although work was well in progress by September 1939, other wartime priorities delayed the opening of the line until the late 1940s.

The major improvements throughout the

system were not confined to passenger facilities. There were numerous alterations to parcels and goods depots, as well as carriage and locomotive sheds, throughout the 1930s, which was thus a busy decade for the Civil Engineer, whose duties also included looking after the existing ways and works. The 'economic' system for maintaining the track on branch lines was extended, and a modest start was made with the provision of power assistance to replace mannual effort in certain routine operations such as boring holes in rails. Electric welding was also adopted to build up parts of worn crossings, and steel keys were tried in replacement of the traditional wooden ones used to hold the rails in the track chairs. Experiments with chemicals to kill weeds were started in 1932, and three years later a special train was constructed for track spraying, made up of three old locomotive tenders and a tank wagon for the chemical concentrate. Mixing and agitation were achieved by the use of steam from the locomotive hauling the train, which could treat up to sixty miles of track in a single day. Another operation involving high-speed chemical reactions was the demolition of various overbridges by explosive in the course of rebuilding.

Mention has already been made of some of the signalling improvements made during the 1930s, but there were two other interesting developments in this period. In 1935, as train speeds started to increase, certain of the distant signals on the line between Paddington and Bristol had to be moved further out to provide greater braking distances, and in certain cases they were worked electrically. The installation of the Great Western Automatic Train Control system was completed to Plymouth, Swansea and Wolverhampton by the end of 1932. The year 1936 marked the start of its further extension, and the final ramp was installed at Penzance in November 1939, completing the coverage of no less than 2,852 miles of main line. Not only was the safety of train operation markedly increased, but in bad visibility trains generally could be kept running far better than on lines not so equipped.

The signal engineers were also active in the 1930s in what we would now refer to as the telecommunications field. The railways had long had their own telegraph systems, and these were being extensively supplemented by telephone circuits. The year 1931 saw the start of carrier-wave transmission on the GWR, initially between Reading and Swindon. This enabled more telephone conversations to be handled over the existing wires. As part of the major improvements that took place, teleprinters finally displaced the last of the single-needle telegraphs at Paddington in 1932, the use of which went back in one form or another for ninety-four years. Paddington also had its own automatic telephone exchange, which was brought into operation in May 1934, and must have proved an invaluable step forward for all those involved in the operation and use of a system that was handling over 12,000 calls per day. Electronics also crept into railway operations via the station loudspeaker systems, the first comprehensive system being that installed at Paddington in 1936. In addition to the use of loudspeakers for passing information to passengers, they proved invaluable when emergency hand-signalling had to be introduced following the electrical fires that occurred in the Paddington Arrival and Westbourne Bridge Signal Boxes in November and December 1938.

The 1930s were thus a very busy period for the Great Western engineering and signal departments, whose efforts in maintaining and improving the infrastructure, as we would now call it, provided the operators with the opportunities to use the Company's locomotives and rolling stock so effectively.

4
Trains and Traffic

Steam traction reached its zenith, so far as speed was concerned, in the 1930s and it was a special source of pride, nationally as well as at Paddington, that for much of this period the Great Western operated the world's fastest train. This was the 'Cheltenham Flyer', as it was popularly known, although its official title was the more prosaic 'Cheltenham Spa Express'. From 1929 it had been scheduled to average 66.2 mph from Swindon to Paddington, making it the fastest scheduled train in the world. Away across the Atlantic, competition between the rival Canadian railways for the Montreal-Toronto traffic resulted in the Canadian Pacific introducing a 68.9 mph schedule in 1931. This eclipsed the Great Western record, and the British company's response came in the September of that year. The 'Cheltenham Flyer's' schedule was cut to sixty-seven minutes, giving a new record average of 69.2 mph start-to-stop, and the introduction of the new timetable provided, as usual, an opportunity to see by how much the schedule could be beaten. As a result 'Launceston Castle' reached Paddington in fractionally under the even hour, corresponding to an average of 77.8 mph, and two days later bettered this by achieving 79.8 mph start-to-stop. This figure even beat the previous world record for the average speed achieved, which had been put up by the Philadelphia & Reading

Railroad back in 1905, and was important enough for *Punch* to devote its main cartoon to the subject. Under the title 'One up to Steam', Frank Reynolds drew an animated version of 'Rocket' waving the union flag and commenting to a *'delighted SHAREHOLDER'* 'EH, LAD, BUT THAT'S CHAMPION!'. Clearly 'Rocket's working career in Lancashire had resulted in its native Geordie accent being overlaid, and one wonders how much this cartoon may have inspired the subsequent anthropomorphic treatment of locomotives in children's stores. There was another delightful cartoon, this time in *The Tatler*, in which H. M. Bateman, in typical style, showed the dire results of 'The man who pulled the communication cord of the "Cheltenham Flyer"'.

Without any additional trans-Atlantic stimulus, the Great Western planned to cut the timing of the 'Flyer' still further in September 1932 to 65 minutes, lifting the booked average over the 70 mph mark for the first time. In preparation for this, a *tour de force* was staged in the previous June, when 'Tregenna Castle', named after the company's own hotel in St Ives, reached Paddington in a mere 56 minutes 47 seconds. This corresponded to an average of 81.7 mph, and set up a record which still remained unbroken in Britain twenty years later.

The 'Cheltenham Flyer' and its achievements

28. On 14 September 1931 the schedule of the 'Cheltenham Flyer' was cut to 67 minutes for the 77¼ miles from Swindon to Paddington, recapturing for Britain and the GWR the prestige of running the 'World's Fastest Train'. 'Launceston Castle' hurtles through Tilehurst at over 80 mph on the inaugural day when the train reached Paddington in just under the even hour.

were undoubtedly a wonderful shop window for the GWR, which were exploited to the maximum with special luggage labels in addition to a headboard proclaiming it as the 'World's Fastest Train'. In retrospect, some of the appeal to the public must have arisen from the time of day at which it ran. It left Swindon just before four and was into Paddington at five in the afternoon, which meant throughout virtually the whole year it arrived before darkness set in, as well as giving tourists plenty of time to get to their hotels, change and wash before an

evening engagement. Unlike the morning high-speed business trains, the passengers would not have been immersed in the preparations for their forthcoming meetings. They could just sit back and watch the scenery of the Thames Valley as they were whisked up to London at over eighty miles an hour, enjoying, if they wished, afternoon tea, although by all accounts the level of liquid in the cups needed to be kept well down. Children going home from school were also able to watch the train's progress from the lineside, and it was only the photographer who was at a disadvantage because of the schedule. Using contemporary materials and equipment one really needed the benefit of good front lighting from the sun, which was not possible with a late afternoon eastbound train.

Although the 'Cheltenham Flyer' was un-

45

29. No 6004 'King George III' hauls the down 'Cornish Riviera Express' past Somerton. The 12-coach train is composed almost entirely of Centenary stock, and the locomotive is carrying the reporting number on its smokebox. The casing for the fire-irons, referred to in the text, can be seen behind the rear pair of driving wheel splashers.

G. H. Soole Collection, National Railway Museum, York

doubtedly the Great Western's show train, it was by no means the only train to be accelerated during the 1930s. All the railway companies were beginning to realise the publicity and commercial advantages of speeding up their services, and the Great Western was well to the fore with these developments. Staggering statistics were produced, such as the reference in the summer of 1932 to the fact that over the previous two years a total of 10,634 minutes a day had been cut from their schedules. More significant

perhaps was that there were then no less than twelve start-to-stop bookings at more than the magic 'mile-a-minute' mark. This was all before the Westbury and Frome cut-offs were opened, and in the following summer the 'Cornish Riviera's' schedule to Plymouth was trimmed to 3 hours 57 minutes. The time of the 'Torbay Express' was also cut by five minutes, and throughout the system a further total of 2,543 minutes was pared from the schedules. The process continued throughout the decade, and by 1938 there were no less than twenty-six start-to-stop schedules at 60 mph or over.

During the 1930s some doubts were cast on the accuracy of the speed record achieved by

30. No 6028 'King George VI' eases a down train off the Westbury avoiding line at Fairwood Junction. This locomotive was renamed in May 1936, having been 'King Henry II' prior to that date.

'City of Truro' in 1904, but in 1939 the Great Western attained a fully-authenticated 100 mph maximum. 'Builth Castle' was timed by R. E. Charlewood, whose original notebooks I now have, to reach a sustained 100 mph through Honeybourne at the foot of Campden Bank on the 12.45 Paddington-Worcester express. By that time, of course, 'Mallard' on the LNER had managed 126 mph while descending Stoke, the culmination of several other runs on the East and West Coast routes when speeds of 100 mph or more had been fully authenticated. Nevertheless, the Great Western probably holds the record for the fastest *pair* of steam-hauled journeys, one in each direction made in quick succession over a given course with similar locomotives, which is rather nearer the con-

ditions that form the basis of any other world speed record. This was in 1932 when, in conjunction with 'Tregenna Castle's' feat on the 'Cheltenham Flyer', two very experienced recorders were invited to make a triple Swindon-Paddington-Swindon-Paddington trip. On the intermediate down journey, 'Manorbier Castle' achieved a timing of 60 minutes and 1 second non-stop to Swindon, which was excellent, as it was against the general rise of the line. The total time for the fastest up journey and the only down trip worked out at 116 minutes 48 seconds, corresponding to an average of 79.4 mph. The recorders in theory only had five minutes to make their connection at Paddington, but the early arrival of the 'Flyer' increased the margin considerably.

Improvements in the Great Western train services during the 1930s were not confined to

47

accelerated schedules, as numerous additional trains were introduced, many of them intended to help cope with the summer Saturday crowds. The year 1934 saw 900 new services being brought into operation, many, of course, being Saturdays-only. In the following year, to mark the completion of the Bristol reconstruction scheme and the company's centenary, the 'Bristolian' was introduced. Intended primarily to appeal to business travellers from London, the morning down train travelled via Bath, while the afternoon return working took the Badminton route. A quarter of an hour was cut from the previous best schedule and the overall averages required were 67.6 mph in the down direction and 67.1 in the up. Initially Kings were rostered to work the new express with its special buffet car, but later on Castles were found to be capable of coping with the schedules.

Another new named express was the 'Cornishman', introduced in 1935. It was, in effect, a second section of the 'Riviera', leaving Paddington five minutes after the premier train, which on Mondays to Fridays was booked to run through to Truro for its first passenger stop. On Saturdays this nominally non-stop run was extended to St Erth, the number of passengers for St Ives and Penzance being enough to fill it. The whole train of 'Centenary' stock was at times worked round to St Ives during the 1930s, where the Tregenna Castle Hotel's minibus would draw up on the platform alongside, in a manner that would do credit to some of the present-day Danish State Railway bus-train interchanges in the Copenhagen area. In 1932 the Great Western introduced a numbering system for trains to and from the West of England on summer Saturdays. Large numerals painted on metal sheets were slotted into frames fixed to the front of the smokebox. The resultant three-figure number was readily visible to signalmen en route as well as other railwaymen directly

CORNWALL GWR

MONTHLY RETURN TICKETS ISSUED ALL THE YEAR ROUND

THE CORNISH RIVIERA" by S.P.B.Mais – Price 1⁺ at G·W·R Stations

National Railway Museum, York

31. A typical GWR poster of the late 1930s, issued after monthly returns had become generally available throughout the whole year.

concerned, who needed to be able to identify which train was which, especially if one was running out of course. The numbers of ordinary booked trains ended in 0 or 5, the system allowing for up to four reliefs to be numbered on consecutively.

It was not solely the long-distance passenger services that were improved in the 1930s. In 1932 the development of the residential area between North Acton and Northolt prompted the building of a new halt at Park Royal, together with the provision of a considerably extended and improved train service on the Ealing-Greenford-Acton triangle. Overnight newspaper trains came in for their share of

LOSTWITHIEL
CHANGE FOR FOWEY

H. C. Casserley

32. No 4907 'Broughton Hall' enters Lostwithiel station with a down train in May 1935.

acceleration too, and 1934 saw speeding up of those to Plymouth and South Wales. The 12.50am train from Paddington to Plymouth was accelerated to the very respectable average of 56.5 mph, but was eclipsed later in the year by the Swansea train, which was scheduled at 58.5 mph to its first stop at Newport. This made it, in its turn, the fastest newspaper train in the world.

During the 1930s passenger trains throughout the GWR averaged fractionally over two minutes late at their destinations, the best year being 1938 when they achieved a figure of 1.95 minutes. However, this overall figure disguises a whole spectrum of individual variations, the 13,000 West of England expresses in 1931, for instance, showing up badly with an average of 8.2 minutes against the all-line figure of 2.4. It was the multitude of local, branch and workmen's trains that helped the overall figures look so good, with boat trains and those conveying perishable traffic below average.

49

33. The wreckage of no 6007 'King William III' after the Shrivenham collision on 15 January 1936. This was one of the rare occasions in which a steam locomotive was so badly damaged in an accident that it had to be replaced, the new one being taken into stock on 24 March of the same year.

There were, of course, set-backs during the decade, the worst individual incident being the Shrivenham collision in January 1936, breaking the twenty-year period when only one other GWR passenger was killed, the record being duly mentioned in the current reports of the accident. Less dramatic, but of considerable long-term economic effect, was the run down of the South Wales collieries and steel industry. In 1931 more than forty of the pits connected with the GWR were closed, with another eighteen working short time. There were some passenger closures over the decade. The Blackmill, Hendreforgan and Gilfach Goch branch, for instance, lost its passenger trains in 1930, as well as the East Street and West Bay stations at Bridport. There was, however, nothing on the GWR comparable to the widespread station closures that took place at that time on the LMS and LNER. Three years later, rationalisation saw the passenger trains over the former Rhondda & Swansea Bay Railway's line at Swansea docks being transferred to the Vale of Neath's tracks. Another of the subsidiary companies of the Western Group did, however, lose its entire

34. Four-wheeled coaching stock was still in use on the Halesowen branch in 1935. The locomotive is no 1524 dating from 1879. Originally built as a saddle tank, it was converted to the pannier variety in 1919, but was still somewhat deficient in cab protection for the footplate crew.

35. The present-day interest in exercise and aerobics had its counterpart half a century ago. In March 1932 the Great Western ran a hikers' mystery express from Paddington which appeared to have attracted a number of enthusiastic, if not too heavily-shod, participants.

passenger service in 1938. This was the former Cleobury Mortimer & Ditton Priors Light Railway, which was, to the end, worked with four-wheeled carriages, specially fitted with additional footboards for use on the low platforms. It is of interest that as early as March 1926 the GWR produced a comprehensive report on reducing the cost of its branch lines, which even considered (but rejected) the idea of turning some into roads for its own lorries and buses. At the other end of the scale, the use of Pullman cars on the GWR had ceased in the autumn of 1930. Although the 'Torbay Pullman' had not proved popular, it was tried on a daily schedule in the summer of that year but then discontinued, along with the use of Pullmans on the Ocean Liner expresses. In the latter connection they were, of course, to be superseded by the GWR's own 'Super Saloons' already referred to in Chapter 2.

As with passengers at holiday periods, the GWR continued to deal with enormous peaks of

British Rail Western Region

36. A milk train at Addison Road in January 1933. The locomotive is Saint no 2973 'Robins Bilitho', and in addition to the United Dairies demountable tank next to the tender, there are four- and six-wheel tank wagons in the train.

37. With St Michael's Mount in the background, broccoli arrives for loading at Penzance. The variety of the type of road transport is matched by the miscellaneous collection of rail vehicles being used.

British Rail Western Region

38. Irish farmers sent over 300 tons of poultry to London for Christmas 1932. Special connecting trains were run from Fishguard to Paddington where one of them is being unloaded in the passenger station.

seasonal fruit and vegetable traffic. In 1931, for instance, the loading bank at St Erth was extended to permit a further ten wagons to be loaded during the broccoli season, and contemporary photographs show how busy the area could be. By 1938 the Cornish traffic as a whole involved just over 22,000 wagons, nearly 30 per cent up on the level achieved four years earlier. Records were also established with the spring flower traffic from the Scilly Isles and with Channel Island tomatoes. Another seasonal business involving the railways was hop-growing, which is usually associated with the Southern Railway and Kent. The Great Western was, however, called on to convey as many as 20,000 pickers to the Herefordshire and Worcestershire areas in a week, many of them from the mining areas of South Wales. Another national product handled at that time in Central Wales was round timber, up to 30,000 tons being forwarded annually. On occasions arrangements were made to load this into wagons on the running lines themselves on Sundays, a hundred or so tons being handled in a single day.

Among the once-off operations carried out by the GWR in the 1930s was the first stage of the move of an entire Cotswold cottage from Chadworth to the United States. Sixty-seven wagons were needed to transport the 475 tons of materials to Brentford, where they were loaded on barges for London Docks. Whether or not this was the original inspiration for the subsequent feature film 'The Ghost Goes West', the GWR was quite extensively involved in filming activities itself in the early 1930s. Their lines and the Manor House Hotel at Moretonhampstead were used in 1931 for the filming of 'The Hound of the Baskervilles'. To show the railways scenes involving Sherlock Holmes, the film company's generating lorry was mounted on a 'Hydra D' wagon at one end of the train and the shooting took place at speeds of up to 40 mph. Later the same month a newsreel was taken of the ATC in action, the camera being mounted on the top of 'Caerphilly Castle's' tender which gave it a clearance of only 4½ inches from some of the overbridges. One of the sequences included shots of a King on an up express running on a parallel track, which involved the film special in speeds of just over 80 mph. Arnold Ridley's play 'The Ghost Train' was also filmed on the GWR in 1931, its general release in the January of the following year being accompanied by 200,000 railway advertising folders 'See the Ghost Train Country'.

Another significant railway film was the one made by the GWR in 1935. It covered the history of the company from the Bristol meeting of 1833 and featured the reproduction 'North

39. From 1929 onwards the Great Western built numbers of new pannier tanks for shunting and other duties. Incorporating numerous standard features, they were much more modern in appearance than their predecessors, such as no 1524 in illustration no 34. No 3731 was one of 50 built at Swindon in 1937. GWR locomotives on regular duties in yards were almost always coupled to a shunter's truck of the type shown.

Star', which was constructed for the centenary celebrations. However, as no broad-gauge tender had been built to go with it, an appropriate standard-gauge one was used instead. Although the fact was disguised by careful filming, the footplate 'crew' had to remember not to step backwards on the side away from the camera. The film was shown in the Physics Theatre of Bristol University after the civic lunch on 31 August that year, and it was also screened at the banquet at Grosvenor House at the end of October, in the presence of the Prince of Wales, the chief guest. A special anniversary number of *The Times* was also printed on 31 August, and at 8pm on the previous evening the BBC National Programme carried an hour-long broadcast entitled 'Great Western Railway 1835–1935, a Programme in Celebration of the Centenary, Devised as a Journey from Paddington to Penzance'. Any member of the company's staff could apply for a free copy of the special number of *The Times*.

40. Making a newsreel of the GWR Automatic Train Control in operation in 1931. The cameraman was perched on the tender of no 4073 'Caerphilly Castle'. This sequence involved filming the King on an up west of England express, with both trains running at over 80 mph.

This account of the Great Western trains and traffic in the 1930s has, of necessity, had to be highly selective, and in order to provide something of an overall view the following table gives an indication of the total originating passenger and freight traffic on the GWR during the period. Journeys by season-ticket holders are excluded.

The total tonnage of freight carried by the GWR was some 30 per cent greater than the quantities originated, while the overall passenger totals, including season ticket holders and non-originating traffic, were about 65 per cent higher than those quoted.

Table 3   TRAFFIC ON THE GREAT WESTERN 1930–39

Year	Originating passenger journeys (million)	Originating freight traffic (million tons)
1930	101.7	60.0
1931	93.2	51.1
1932	89.8	48.5
1933	90.0	48.4
1934	91.9	50.4
1935	93.7	50.6
1936	93.5	50.3
1937	95.5	56.3
1938	88.2	49.4
1939	84.5	53.7

Source: Great Western Railway General Statistics, October 1941

5
Docks and Marine Activities

As described in the first part of this work, the GWR had become the largest dock-owner in the world in the 1920s, with the main concentration of its activity in the Welsh ports along the northern shore of the Bristol Channel. This was one of the worst-hit areas in Britain during and after the Great Depression. The Great Western's dock activities suffered in sympathy, and already in 1929 steps had been taken to close one of the docks. This was the Town Dock at Newport, and one of the clauses in the Great Western Railway Act of 1929 gave the company authority to do this. Closure accordingly took place in the autumn of 1930, and was permanent. A year later the plans of the area showed various buildings and land available for letting, while there was the ominous note: 'The Inner Basin of the Town Dock is closed, and cannot be entered by vessels. Vessels which enter the Outer Basin (which is continuously open to the River) do so entirely at their own risk.' The Town Dock facilities were, however, relatively small compared with the others in the area, but worse was to occur later in the 1930s.

Business in the South Wales docks had fallen from a total of 44 million tons in 1923 to 35 million tons in 1930, and then continued to drop

still further to a level of 25 million five years later. With a decrease of a further 13 per cent during the first half of 1936, something drastic had to be done, since the net revenue from the Great Western's dock undertakings had dropped from £545,000 in 1939 to a mere £47,000 in 1935. The sanctions imposed on Italy, following their invasion of Abyssinia, had alone cost two million tons a year of Welsh coal, while earlier the effect of reparation coal deliveries from Germany, and the elimination of coal-burning ships from the Royal Navy, had also played their part. The idea of closing Penarth Dock had been mooted in 1932 but local representations had persuaded the railway to keep it going, while the Plymouth Estates had agreed to forgo their royalties for the time being. All these measures were not enough, however, and in 1936 it was decided to close the Dock *temporarily*, leaving the Tidal Harbour still available. Ship owners wishing to lay up ships could use the dock and access was still available to the privately-owned ship-repairing facilities inside the dock, in which, however, the GWR had a financial interest. Penarth Dock was nearly 3,000 feet in length, compared with a mere 900 for the inner basin at Newport Town, and was extensively

British Rail Western Region

41. Rebuilding of the quay wall on the Weymouth tramway in September 1938. The girder bridge taking the railway to Portland is situated on the far side of the harbour beyond the miscellaneous vessels moored to the quay.

equipped with coal loading facilities, four of them being capable of lifting twenty-ton wagons to a height of 60 feet for discharge.

Although these closures overshadowed the Great Western's dock activities in South Wales during the 1930s, there were numerous improvements constantly being made to their facilities throughout the decade, in addition to all the routine maintenance works. For example, 1930 saw the provision of a 'ferro-concrete' timber stage at Newport North Dock, complete with nine hydraulic cranes. Belt conveyors were installed at Cardiff in the following years, and there were other changes in the loading equipment. One of these was the use of anti-breakage conveyors to lower coal into ships' holds rather more gently than a normal chute did, while

'Norfolk' diggers or spades were fitted extensively to assist the discharge of duff and other grades of small coal from the up-ended wagons. The necessity for the latter was perhaps indicative of a falling quality of Welsh coal. Extra charges were made by the railway for the use of each of these types of equipment. The Mumbles lighthouse, owned and operated by the railway, was converted from oil to electricity in 1935. Improvements were made to some of the cattle lairages, this particular traffic being one which had its ups and downs. In 1931, for instance, the first-ever import of animals from Rhodesia helped to compensate for the cessation of Irish operations because of an outbreak of foot and mouth disease in Pembrokeshire. There was an improvement in the Canadian cattle movements; the trade was switched to Halifax from the St Lawrence where it had been interrupted by the freeze each winter. A new twin-screw tug was provided at Cardiff in 1931, taking over the name 'The Earl' from its predecessor, which was renamed 'GWR 127' prior to being sold. A second similar vessel, 'Windsor', was ordered for use at Barry later the same year, which replaced a pair of earlier vessels there.

From the passengers' point of view, the most significant change in the decade was the major rebuilding of Weymouth Pier in 1932–33. Traffic there had built up considerably over the years, to the point at which the GWR was paying no less than £10,000 per annum in harbour dues. Beyond the Palm Court and the Pavilion Theatre, the old wooden structure had tapered very drastically, permitting only a maximum of four coaches to be berthed in the platform. The new reinforced concrete pier, over three times the width of the old one, carried a pair of tracks which, with their new platforms, could accommodate no less than thirty-six coaches. On the north side, away from the harbour, there was a public promenade with shelters which themselves had flat promenade roofs. The main harbour works were financed by the town, with railway guarantees. One passenger and three cargo vessels could be moored simultaneously alongside the railway tracks and the six new cranes, with space for two more pleasure vessels further out. The plans for the whole of the pier and buildings were prepared by the railway and the formal opening by the Prince of Wales took place in July 1933.

It was to be a further five years, however, before the problems of the tramway from the main station to the pier were dealt with. The sharp curve at Ferry's Corner, which had necessitated the use of special couplings on bogie coaches, was eliminated by building a new piled quay wall out into the river on the upstream side. This very closely followed the plan put forward as long before as 1862, when a viaduct had been proposed on much the same alignment. Progress of the boat trains was still, of necessity, very slow through the streets, but no longer were there the time-consuming shunting movements. A quick change of locomotive from dock tank to Castle saw the express away up the bank past Upwey Wishing Well Halt after a stop of under seven minutes. The final planned improvement to the railway facilities at Weymouth was announced in the summer of 1939. It involved the reconstruction of the Town station with a fine new building and extra platform space to deal with the 1¼ million passengers arriving every year, but work was held up by the war.

Out on the short-sea crossings themselves, the Great Western's fleet continued to provide services to and from Ireland and the Channel Islands. The 'St Julien' and 'St Helier' maintained their yeoman service on the latter route from Weymouth, being extensively modernised at Penarth, ready for the 1937 season. Greater space was provided for third-class passengers under cover, together with improved first-class accommodation and additional feeding facilities. On each vessel twenty-two extra berths were provided, while the number of seats available, exclusive of those in dining areas, was increased by a factor of five to 195. From 1930 the two older vessels were supplemented on the Channel Islands service during the summer by the 'St Patrick', a new twin-turbine vessel of 1922 tons. During the winter, she was switched to the Fishguard-Rosslare service.

The 'St Patrick' was the first of the new generation of ships to be built for the Irish traffic, and replaced her 1906 predecessor. Two years later the 'St David' and 'St Andrew' were also replaced. Although operated by the Great Western, they were owned by a subsidiary, the Fishguard & Rosslare Railways & Harbours Co, and were turbine-powered. A clause in the contract with the builders stipulated that steel from South Wales was to be used for their construction. They boasted a ladies' lounge 'tastefully decorated and upholstered in restful shades, the furniture being of walnut'. Finally in 1934 a fourth new ship, the 'Great Western' entered service on the Fishguard-Waterford ser-vice. She had only triple-expansion reciprocating engines and was the first British vessel to be built with fully-mechanised coal-firing equipment for the boilers. She was capable of carrying over 660 head of cattle, and replaced the 'Great Southern', which had operated the service for thirty years, together with the earlier 'Great Western' of 1902.

The ocean liner business at Plymouth continued to be a very important one for the GWR during the 1930s, and in 1931 a new tender arrived for service there. She was the 'Sir Richard Grenville', replacing the forty-year-old ship of the same name, and similar to the 'Sir John Hawkins', which had started work in 1929. During the design stages, consideration was given to the use of a diesel-electric drive on the new tender as well as with the 'St Andrew' and 'St David'. As already mentioned these two were finally equipped with steam turbines, while the propulsion demands of the smaller tender in the end only justified triple-expansion reciprocating engines, which had the advantage that the whole of the passenger accommodation could be heated by steam in the winter months. She and the Rosslare ships were oil-fired, so there seem to have been plenty of design options available for propulsion and steam-generation at that time. A dining saloon was provided on 'Sir Richard Grenville' for use on excursion trips along the Devon and Cornish coasts in the summer, during lulls between the calls of ocean liners.

In the 1920s the Great Western's shipping activities were run at a loss, although the overall deficit was rapidly being reduced at the end of that decade. The loss in 1929 was only £1,200, but this had become a profit of £2,600 in 1930. Thereafter the balance from the marine activities rose to £23,500 in 1938. This corresponded to an operating ratio of 93 per cent, which was, however, appreciably less attractive than the corresponding LMS figure of 85, while the SR managed to get down to 74 per cent on receipts of over £1.5m. This provides a very clear indication of the commercial advantage of the short Channel crossings exploited so successfully by the Southern, while the London Midland & Scottish was able to profit from its routes which served the capitals of Eire and Northern Ireland so much more directly.

The finances of the Great Western's dock activities were saved by the drastic surgery of 1936, and, as a result of cutting the working expenses that year by £125,000, they succeeded in raising the balance from £47,000 in 1935 to £120,000. Clearly if the slide had been allowed to continue the whole of their dock operations

Photo Source Fox

42. Pannier tank no 2195 'Cwm Mawr' eases a boat train through the streets of Weymouth en route to the pier. Railway flagmen stop road traffic on the cross-road. The locomotive was built for the Burry Port & Gwendreath Valley Railway in 1905 by the Avonside Engine Co, and was one of two that migrated to Weymouth after the Grouping.

would have been in the red. With the subsequent improvement in receipts the balances looked somewhat more healthy in later years, but were still well below the figures for the 1920s, with the exception of the General Strike year of 1926. The LMS and LNER dock activities were not doing very well either in the 1930s, the former's frequently being in deficit, while the net balance from the LNER's operations fell drastically. It was only the Southern, which had invested heavily in new facilities, especially at Southampton, that retained a percentage operating ratio in the healthy low seventies throughout, in spite of its receipts being only about two-thirds of those of the GWR. There seemed little doubt

by the late 1930s that the Great Western's docks were no longer ideally situated, nor were they equipped for the most profitable cargo and passenger flows.

For the sake of completeness, mention should be made by way of a postscript to the Great Western's other water-borne activities – its canals. Like those of the LNER and LMS they lost money steadily throughout the 1930s. Only the Southern's remained profitable, when, with just one mile remaining open in 1938 expenses were £804 compared with receipts of £1,750. The only canals owned by the GWR that were in surplus in 1939, apart from the Swansea Canal, were those at Kensington and Stover, and all of their respective lengths of 33 chains and 2 miles were in fact leased to outside companies. The age of the inland waterway appeared to be over by the end of the 1930s, certainly so far as those owned by the railways were concerned.

6

Road Transport

Although, so far as road transport is concerned, this book is primarily concerned with the Great Western Railway's own road fleet and operations, we cannot ignore the general competitive development of road transport throughout the 1930s, which was the subject of much contemporary debate. The Royal Commission on Transport produced the third and last of its reports in January 1931. Following these there was much activity by all those with vested interests of one sort or another, but new legislation was introduced which had considerable effect on the development of road operations. These regulations can be summarised as covering two very different aspects.

The first of these fields of regulation, already extensively incorporated in the 1930 Road Traffic Act, concerned what we would today refer to as the construction and usage aspects of the vehicles. They were vitally necessary on safety grounds to curb the rapidly-growing accident rate and to ensure the fitness of the vehicles, heavy ones particularly, for the roads of the time. Third-party insurance was made compulsory, speed limits imposed, and driving tests were ultimately introduced. Solid tyres were frowned on in favour of pneumatics, and widespread conversions of older railway-owned road vehicles took place. Advantages were also to be gained from the lower weight that re-

sulted, which put the vehicle into a cheaper licensing bracket. Some horse-drawn vehicles were similarly modernised by the GWR in the late 1930s, and they were even provided with electric lighting in addition to being fitted with drum brakes in place of the traditional block operating on the steel rim of the solid wooden wheel. The safety regulations were open-ended and even today new requirements are constantly being introduced in the interests of safety as vehicle speeds and weights continue to increase. Another example of this, not long before World War II, was the need to fit safety glass windscreens, a feature we now take very much for granted. As part of the general tightening up of the skills required by heavy vehicle drivers, the Great Western opened its own training school, situated immediately south of the main-line at Taplow.

No one would really have argued with the need to bring in new road safety measures of the sort just outlined, but there remained a wide divergence between the road and rail attitudes to the quantity licensing arrangements that followed the Royal Commission's third report and the subsequent 1933 Road Traffic Act. This stipulated that all road haulage vehicles, over a certain weight, had to obtain one of three categories of licence. A C Licence permitted the vehicle's owner to carry only his own goods,

43. In 1931 the Great Western Railway placed the largest-ever single order for road vehicles. Messrs J Thornycroft & Co undertook to supply the chassis for one hundred 30-cwt vehicles and a similar number of 4-tonners. One batch is shown lined up outside the firm's Basingstoke Works, ready for delivery in November 1931.

while at the other end of the scale the general haulage contractor operated under an A Licence. The intermediate category B Licence covered vehicles used primarily for the owner's own goods but they could also be used, under certain specified conditions, for general haulage 'for hire or reward'. Existing operators in 1933 were automatically granted licences for what were, in effect, the vehicles they already owned, but all additional vehicles subsequently acquired involved an appropriate application to the Traffic Commissioners. They had to decide whether there was a genuine need for additional capacity, and other interested parties could put forward their objections, which the railways naturally did, almost as a matter of course.

None of these moves, however, removed the one great difficulty as far as the railways were concerned. Their haulage rates were fixed by statutory tribunals and Acts of Parliament, and could not be varied to benefit from any particularly valuable traffic that might be in the offing. Furthermore their actual rates had to be published, including any that had been preferentially reduced. At the beginning of the 1930s they could not drop their rates by more than five per cent without a formal application, but that

44. The stationmaster at Lechlade supervises the transfer of sacks from one of the GWR's Thornycroft lorries into store in January 1935.

freedom was subsequently given to them, although the actual figures were still available to anyone interested. Another useful freedom the railways obtained in the 1930s was the ability to quote an overall rate of so much per ton for the country-wide distribution of a firm's products. There had even been an expensive legal case in the early 1930s to challenge the railway's legality to do this, a case which the railways had actually lost, and the Great Western quickly took advantage of the newly-won right. The railway even provided road vehicles in a firm's livery for the distribution of its products from a railhead, and, if required, the driver could also be kitted out in the firm's own uniform. Distribution depots were also established, where necessary, on railway property, for storage purposes in connection with such schemes.

None of these rate restrictions applied to the road hauliers, which, furthermore, had no common-carrier liability like the railways, who had to be prepared to take anything, however awkward, that could be got on a railway wagon within the confines of the loading gauge. The quantity licensing restrictions did not, however, prevent a serious continuing inroad being made into railway revenues, and this led to the 'Square Deal Campaign' launched in late 1938. The railways sought early legislative steps to the effect that:

45. The Great Western's road training school in action in April 1936. The original caption for this photograph by the Topical Press stated 'One of the tests for the learner. A pedestrian walks across the road reading a newspaper and the driver *has* to pull up.'

(a) The existing statutory regulation of the charges for the conveyance of merchandise traffic by railway, together with the requirements attached thereto, including such matters as classification, publication and undue preference should be repealed.

(b) The railways would be authorised to make such charges for conveyance, etc of merchandise, and to attach thereto such conditions as they think fit.

This request, to enable them to compete on equal commercial terms with road hauliers, was backed up by the short public statement shown.

In the event no such Bill was presented to Parliament, let alone an Act passed, but the looming clouds of war were to force some degree of cooperation between the railways and road haulage interests. This led to national and regional road-rail committees, the existence of which was to prove invaluable for totally different purposes after war had been declared.

To turn to the Great Western's own road operations, it was ironic that one of the results of the quantity licensing regulations which had been brought in to curb runaway competition not only necessitated them having to apply for many new licences of their own, but cost them at least £30,000 per year more. This was a result of the reorganised scales of vehicle taxation following the 1937 Finance Act. The GWR was by no means constrained by these changes to cut

G. H. Soole Collection, National Railway Museum, York

46. Upstairs, Downstairs. Out of sight of the passengers using the imposing entrance to Temple Meads station in Bristol is a selection of the jointly-owned GWR–LMS cartage fleet. The vehicle on the far left is one of the Thornycroft type shown in illustration no 43.

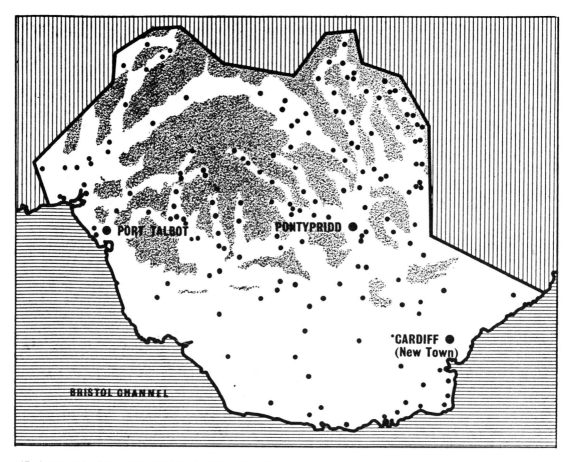

PORT TALBOT

PONTYPRIDD

CARDIFF ●
(New Town)

BRISTOL CHANNEL

47. An example of the way in which the handling of goods
traffic was rationalised in the inter-war years. Prior to 1927
there were no less than 156 stations in this area of South
Wales that dealt with general goods traffic.

back on its own investment in road haulage
vehicles, some of which, it should be noted,
carried loads from one point to another without
going anywhere near a railway wagon. In 1934,
for instance, it announced orders for no less
than 396 new motor vehicles, at a cost of
£156,500, 'for the development of its cartage
services and replacements'. At the end of 1939
their fleet comprised 2,450 motor vehicles and
2,164 trailers, with a handful of jointly-owned

vehicles in addition. With the latter great care
was taken to see that no undue preference was
given to one company; so vans were marked
'GWR & LMS' on one side and 'LMS & GWR'
on the other. The initials were similarly reversed
between the front and back. Space on the sides of
covered vans was also allocated for the display of
'Quad Royal' posters, so that the vehicles became mobile bill-boards for the railways' own
services or the products of their customers.

The 1930s were a period of considerable
technical development with road transport, and
the GWR was quick to adopt any worthwhile

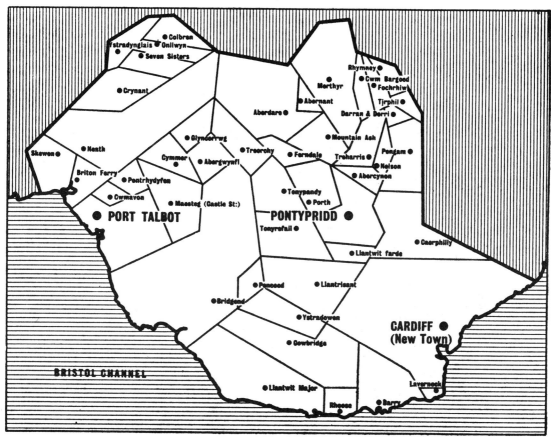

On the map the following place names appear:

Colbren, Onllwyn, Ystradynglais, Seven Sisters, Crynant, Rhymney, Merthyr, Cwm Bargoed, Fochrhiw, Tirphil, Abernant, Darran & Deri, Aberdare, Skewen, Neath, Glyncorrwg, Treorchy, Mountain Ash, Pengam, Cymmer, Abergwynfi, Ferndale, Treharris, Nelson, Briton Ferry, Pontrhydyfen, Abercynon, Cwmavon, Maesteg (Castle St:), Tonypandy, Porth, **PORT TALBOT**, **PONTYPRIDD**, Tonyrefail, Caerphilly, Llantwit fardre, Pencoed, Llantrisant, Bridgend, Ystradowen, **CARDIFF (New Town)**, Cowbridge, **BRISTOL CHANNEL**, Laverneck, Llantwit Major, Rhoose, Barry

48. Following the GWR's reorganisation of its goods traffic arrangements in 1927, there was a drastic reduction in the number of stations handling general traffic of this sort. The operations were concentrated in just forty-six stations, each of them serving its own area by means of road deliveries and collections.

innovations. The most significant of these was the articulated principle, which was widely used from the early 1930s onwards. At the bottom of the scale, the three-wheel 'Karrier Kobs' and Scammell 'Mechanical Horses' were admirable substitutes for the short-range horse-drawn delivery vehicle, and retained much of the latter's manoeuvrability. This was a vital characteristic for use in crowded shopping streets with their plethora of small individual shops. The GWR also purchased seven 'Karrier Kobs' in 1932 to assist horse-drawn vehicles up the hill outside Hockley goods depot in Birmingham, where they replaced the chain horses used hitherto, and some were even used to tow former horse-drawn vehicles, at least inside large goods depots. The quickly-detachable trailers used on these short-range articulated delivery services had other advantages from the railways' point of view, as the expensive power unit and its driver could be used elsewhere while loading or unloading of the trailer took place. The railways' house removal services used this principle very

67

49. A campaign in depth. A Square Deal campaign banner spans the road at the exit from the arrival platforms at Paddington, while a visiting Southern Railway van proclaims the same message. Behind the van are the Arrival Side Offices constructed as part of the 1930s rebuilding of the station.

extensively, and where railway employees were concerned the container was provided and moved free, but the loading and unloading was the responsibility of the householder. Visually the standard B or BK containers sat much more securely on articulated trailers than they did on some of the earlier rigid vehicles used, which appeared to be in imminent danger of tipping up backwards. At the end of the decade, the threat of petrol shortages during any hostilities led

to the GWR experimenting with articulated vehicles powered by producer gas.

The availability of satisfactory road delivery vehicles enabled considerable economies to be made in railway operations by concentrating small consignments to a much more limited section of stations. The diagrams show how this development took place in the valleys of South Wales, with traffic being gradually concentrated on 46 of the original 156 stations that had been handling it in 1927. Even though arrangements of this sort were carried out over the whole country, the railways as a whole still lost heavily on their collection and delivery services during the 1930s. From an annual deficit of £269,000 for the GWR in 1929, the figure dropped to £123,000 in 1934, only to climb again to much the same original level at the end of the decade, by which time the revenue was only contributing four-fifths of the cost of the operations. Only the Southern managed to keep its collection and delivery operations in the black, the performance of the other three groups being very similar on a percentage basis, probably reflecting their greater involvement in the industrial areas of the country.

In October 1933 the four railway companies purchased the whole of the ordinary shares of two major road haulage firms: Carter Paterson and Hay's Wharf Cartage, the latter being better known as Pickfords. The holdings were shared between the railways, and by 1939 the Great Western's capital involvement and incomes from the two companies were as follows:

Table 4 GREAT WESTERN RAILWAY OWNERSHIP OF CARTAGE COMPANIES IN 1939

Company	Investment (£)	Dividends etc received in 1939 (£)	Return (%)
Carter Paterson & Co. Ltd	335,749	14,963	4.5
Hay's Wharf Cartage Co. Ltd	210,059	24,737	11.8
	545,808	39,700	7.3

Source: GWR Annual Report

Table 5 GREAT WESTERN PASSENGER ROAD TRANSPORT INVESTMENT IN 1939

Company	Investment (£)	Dividends received in 1939 (£)	Return (%)
Birmingham & Midland Motor Omnibus Co. Ltd	411,500	42,000	10.2
City of Oxford Motor Services Ltd	123,868	12,469	10.1
Crosville Motor Services Ltd	148,212	10,988	7.4
Devon General Omnibus and Touring Co. Ltd	62,945	5,115	8.1
Thames Valley Traction Co. Ltd	93,710	9,220	9.8
Western National Omnibus Co. Ltd	1,263,378	116,308	9.2
Western Welsh Omnibus Co. Ltd	196,520	32,415	16.5
	2,300,133	228,515	9.9

Source: GWR 1939 Annual Report

69

The variation in the rates of return reflects the different types of business with which each company was involved, Carter Paterson being primarily a collection and delivery firm. On the other hand, Pickfords, whose origins dated back to the days of Charles I, were in the heavy haulage end of the market as well as house removals.

As we saw in Volume 1, the GWR's passenger road operations were at the end of the 1920s being progressively transferred to its associated bus companies. The process continued during the early 1930s, and 1934 saw the end of the Great Western's own operations, by which time the associated companies were running a total of 3,500 buses. The last of the GWR's services was the one used to transfer continental passengers between Paddington and Victoria, and was taken over by the London Passenger Transport Board, while the two buses the GWR had used were converted to delivery lorries. By the end of the decade the Great Western's investments in these road passenger services had become remarkably profitable, as the figures in Table 2 show, although they pale beside the LNER's twenty-two per cent return from the United Automobile Services. Some of the ownership arrangements were fairly complicated, involving investment by more than one railway in a given omnibus company, while in 1936 the Royal Blue long-distance services were taken over by the Western and Southern National companies. Today's deregulated National coach services to the west of England thus include a long period of railway involvement in their ancestry. In the 1930s, however, that threat lay well over the horizon and the Great Western benefited very considerably from its associated

---

The Railways ask for a Square Deal.

MUCH is being said about the poor financial position of the Railway Industry.

The real position can be stated in a few short sentences.

1. In fixing rates and conditions for carrying merchandise the Railways are bound by statutory controls and regulations which have lasted a hundred years and grown more rigid with age.

2. No other form of goods transport is subject to such restrictions or anything comparable with them.

3. Moreover, no other form of transport has or can have such basic duties and responsibilities to the State as those which the Railways must bear at all times, and more especially in times of national emergency.

4. It will be impossible for the Railways adequately to discharge those national services and duties unless they are allowed now to put their house in order, and to run their business on business lines.

5. The Railways have no desire whatsoever to interfere with other transport services or with any other business.

6. They merely want the chance to put themselves right so that they may be able to meet fair competition in a fair way. The main transport services should all start equal.

7. The time-honoured shackles which fetter the Railways alone, and well-nigh strangle their goods traffic, must go.

8. And they must go before it is too late.

9. A short Act of Parliament must be passed this Session to meet a crying national need.

50. The details of the railways Square Deal campaign.

road passenger operations. Through booking arrangements were also available with the associated companies for parcels traffic, while considerable advantage was taken of the inter-availability arrangements for passenger tickets, to everyone's advantage.

7
Eating, Drinking and Sleeping

While the railways may have had diffi- culty in making ends meet with their collection and delivery services during the 1930s, the same was certainly not the case with their catering and hotel activities. Passengers were prepared to pay the full cost of the refresh- ment services on trains and stations, and the railways' own hotels successfully managed to maintain their profitability.

Although there was a steady programme of construction of new catering vehicles through- out the 1930s, there were only three innovations of note. These were the introduction of Quick Lunch Bar cars in 1934, followed by the more- familiar buffet cars two years later, and the provision of full air conditioning on a restaurant/kitchen pair in 1935. Only two of the Quick Lunch Bar cars were built, and they had a bar counter running down the centre of the vehicle for virtually its full length. Passengers sat up to this on high stools, and the windows behind them were set higher than normal to maintain a satisfactory sight-line, while those behind the bar were of frosted glass. One was used in the 'Bristolian' after its introduction in 1935. British Railways preserved one of them,

which was displayed at Clapham. It passed into the care of the National Railway Museum and is currently on loan to the Severn Valley Railway.

The last pre-war batch of five buffet cars, built in 1938, ran on six-wheel bogies and had exter- nal dimensions that permitted them to operate fairly freely throughout the country, away from the more-generous GWR loading gauge. They were finished internally in two alternative styles. The panelling was either bleached teak or wal- nut, with green moquette or red leather uphol- stery, the whole effect being much cosier than the standards we have become used to over the last couple of decades. Some stools were pro- vided around the bar counter which would certainly not be an acceptable feature in most of today's InterCity buffet cars with their queues waiting to be served. An 'intercom' was pro- vided to enable the steward on the counter to relay instructions to the kitchen area. One of these vehicles was repainted in chocolate and cream in 1956 when that livery was restored for the 'Bristolian', remaining at work on that train until 1961, ten years after the first of the British railways standard coaches had appeared. Buffet facilities were also incorporated in various of the

51. A contrast in buffet cars I. In July 1932 a gas-lit clerestory coach no 9516 provides the buffet facilities on a Paddington–Oxford train.

streamlined railcars designed for express work, as instanced by no 4, which is part of the National Collection.

Although the LNER's 'Silver Jubilee' stock was pressure-ventilated, no provision was made for actually cooling the air in the summer. The first proper installation of this sort was in the pair of GWR vehicles nos 9640 and 9642 which appeared with a complete absence of fuss in 1935, and were not even used on prestige trains. They could be distinguished by grilles on the body-sides and a flexible air duct connecting the two vehicles above the ordinary gangway connection. No sliding ventilators were provided on the windows, which also provided a quick visual distinction, although in 1948 they acquired them when they were refurbished. The cooling was provided by an ice-box, holding 19 cwt, mounted on the underframe, as with the LMS's 1941 Royal saloons.

As train speeds have increased in the last two decades and passengers have become more fitness-conscious, there has been a noticeable change in the demands made for on-rail catering. We should be careful therefore not to imagine that restaurant cars were quite so re-

52. A contrast in buffet cars II. Four years later the Great Western had built this buffet-third no 9644.

stricted to the executive traveller as they tend to be today. Passengers on excursions to the Newbury races, for instance, expected to have a full luncheon on the train on the way down to the racecourse station, which is only fifty-two miles from London. Each of the open excursion sets mentioned in Chapter 2 was provided with a pair of kitchen cars to enable meals to be served to every seat on specials such as these. While we associate full restaurant car meals with 'Silver Service', this was actually introduced on the GWR in 1937 as part of a general revamp of their catering arrangements, which included 'à la carte breakfasts, extended and more varied menus, and abridged meals at reduced prices to suit the pockets of all and sundry'. In the usual annual review of the company's activities in the following January issue of the *Great Western Railway Magazine*, special tribute was paid 'to the efforts of the entire restaurant car staff to make these improvements the success they have proved. The staff have mastered the intricacies of changed and somewhat trying conditions, and they have borne then with an invariably smiling cheerfulness'. For the record, while there is a silver service on the British section of the 'Venice Simplon-Orient Express', over on the mainland of Europe dinner is presented in 'nouvelle cuisine' style, the plates being prepared in the kitchens. This emphasises the variations in restaurant car traditions in different countries.

The Great Western's hotel business in the 1930s continued along the lines established during the previous decade. During holiday periods

73

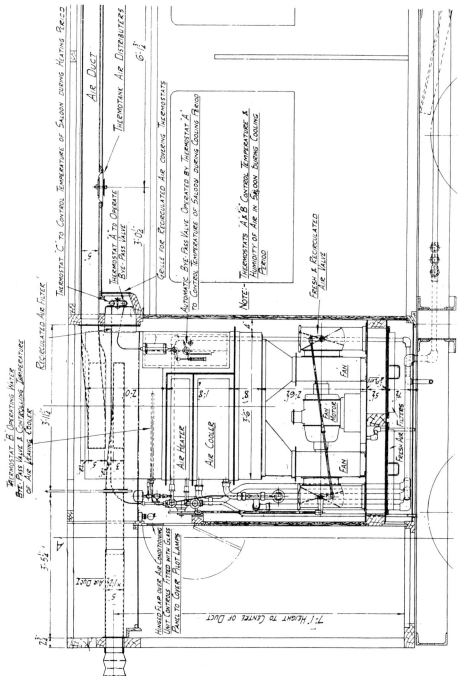

Thermostat "B" Operating Water Bye-Pass Valve & Controlling Temperature of Air Leaving Cooler

Recirculated Air Filter

Thermostat "C" to Control Temperature of Saloon during Heating Period

Air Duct

Thermotank Air Distributers

6·1½

3·0½

Thermostat "A" to Operate Bye-Pass Valve

Grille for Recirculated Air covering Thermostats

Automatic Bye-Pass Valve Operated by Thermostat "A" to Control Temperature of Saloon during Cooling Period

Note:— Thermostats "A" & "B" Control Temperature & Humidity of Air in Saloon during Cooling Period

Fresh & Recirculated Air Valve

Air Heater

Air Cooler

Fan

Fan Motor

Fan

Fresh Air Filters

Hinged Flap over Air Conditioning Unit Controls Fitted with Glass Panel to Cover Pilot Lamps

Air Duct

7·1½ Height to Centre of Duct

3·5½

2·3

53. The original Swindon drawing showing the air conditioning equipment in the GWR restaurant car no 9640. It occupied *National Railway Museum, York* the space between the corridor and the right-hand side of the vehicle, which had louvres in it to admit fresh air. The pipes running along the underframe to the right conveyed water to and from the ice box underneath the centre of the vehicle. Air for the second car passed through the flexible duct at the top left, positioned over the normal corridor connection.

the Tregenna Castle and Manor House Hotels were always full, and there were extensions to both in 1934 and 1935 respectively. The latter comprised the addition of a further thirty-six additional bedrooms, each with its own bathroom, and a new dining room. The Tregenna Castle extension was more modest, with eleven new bedrooms on a new floor above the west wing, but the same number of additional lock-up garages was provided, indicative of the changing modes of transport used by holiday-makers.

At Paddington the Great Western Hotel was receiving almost constant extension or refurbishment during the 1930s. Work started on a

54. The luxury of the third-class restaurant car built as part of the Cornish Riviera Centenary Stock.

55. The attractively-designed open excursion stock introduced in 1935. When used on Newbury race specials, a full luncheon would be served to every seat on the train during the fifty-two mile journey from Paddington.

56. Building work in progress at the Manor House Hotel in January 1935.

completely new wing in 1935, and the whole scheme included a complete reconstruction of the exterior. Considerable engineering work was required to carry out the alterations because of the various railway facilities underneath it. Down at the Fishguard Bay Hotel, which was operated but not owned by the GWR, work started in 1938 on a modernisation scheme, but the hoped-for additional patronage did not immediately materialise. The remaining hotels owned by the GWR, the George & Railway at Bristol, the Great Western at Taunton, and the Marine at Penarth Docks, were leased and need not concern us here.

Mention has been made in Chapter 3 of the proposed hotel at Looe, but this was overshadowed in size by the plans, announced in 1939, for one at Snow Hill in Birmingham. It was to have been constructed as part of the railway station complex, taking the place of the divisional offices and restaurant, with frontages in Colmore Row and Livery Street as well as Snow Hill itself. The seven-storey block would have accommodated 28 double and 142 single rooms, each with its own bathroom. According to the published drawings, it was externally much more contemporary in appearance than the GWR's reconstructed hotel at Paddington. The facings of Portland stone and some of the detailing have quite a degree of similarity to the LMS's new hotel, the Queen's at Leeds, which had been opened in 1937. Had it been built, it would certainly have been a major and imposing addition to the Great Western's presence in Birmingham.

At many stations during the 1930s there was a general refurbishing programme for the restaurant and refreshment rooms, particularly when a major rebuilding programme was taking place. It is interesting to note that it was necessary in those days for the company to make provision for the accommodation of its refreshment staff at large stations. As part of the general reconstruction of railway facilities in the Paddington area, a new hostel was built on the fourth and fifth floors of the new Stationery Department's headquarters alongside Westbourne Bridge in 1934, with seventy single bedrooms for the female Refreshment Department staff at the station. With its communal rooms overlooking the west end of London it must have been one of the earliest and largest penthouse suites. The staff house at Exeter was similarly reconstructed in 1938.

Throughout the 1930s the Great Western was able to maintain an operating ratio close to the ninety per cent mark for its hotels, refreshment rooms and cars, a performance that was much in line with the other companies', although the general level of their business was a great deal smaller than that on the LMS and LNER. The annual receipts of those companies were about £3 million and £2 million respectively, compared with £¾ million for the GWR and less than £150,000 for the Southern. As an ancillary to their main business of rail transport, it was nevertheless useful to be able to make a profit, rather than have to decide how large a deficit to budget for as a 'loss leader'.

8
Taking to the Air

The British railway companies had a long tradition of involvement in other modes of transport, and it was not perhaps surprising that the development of air services in the early 1930s should interest and involve the railway companies. Even in the days before World War I, excursions had been run by the railways to events such as the Doncaster Air Races, but commercial airline operations were another matter altogether. It was not until the late 1920s that this was seen as a potential opportunity (or threat) by the British railways, and they quickly obtained Parliamentary powers to operate air services in 1929. Having done this they then sat back and waited until the time was ripe to utilise them, the GWR having carried out some detailed examinations which showed there was no immediate scope.

In spite of the depression, domestic air services started in Britain in 1932, and the railways decided to make a move, but the GWR, with typical technical initiative, was in first and on its own, a year before the formation of the jointly-owned Railway Air Services. The route chosen was from Cardiff to Haldon (near Newton Abbot and Teignmouth) and Roborough (for Plymouth), which gave a much shorter route than the railway via the Severn Tunnel, because of the Bristol Channel. The scheduled flying time from Cardiff to Haldon was fifty minutes,

so that, allowing for bus transfers at each end, the road-air-road time from the centre of Cardiff to Plymouth was about three hours faster than by rail. A three-engined Westland Wessex, complete with personalised registration G–AAGW, was chartered from Imperial Airways for the service, and duly painted in chocolate and cream, while the GWR's coat of arms appeared on the rudder. The aircraft had six seats only and two round trips a day were operated initially.

The inauguration of the service was carried out in typical Great Western style on 11 April. A luncheon was held at Cardiff during which a message was read from Lord Londonderry, the Secretary of State for Air, in which he referred to:

The initiative of the Great Western Railway in undertaking this new venture will be welcomed by the whole flying world, and may well prove to be the beginning of far-reaching developments in co-operative transport for the mutual benefit of rail and air communication.

After these festivities the large party left for the airport and watched the service aircraft leave with its six passengers, including S. B. Collett, the GWR Assistant Secretary and a qualified

57. A Railway Air Services aircraft loads Richmond sausages at Liverpool on 29 May 1934. 1934 was the first year of RAS operation, and the aircraft operated a round trip from Liverpool to Plymouth with intermediate stops, but the destinations of the sausages were not recorded.

pilot, whose initiative and knowledge had materially contributed to the project. The service arrived at Haldon in forty-four minutes, 'at times reaching a speed of 120 miles per hour', and it was accompanied by another similar aircraft conveying directors and others to assist at the various civic receptions after arrival in Devon. An appreciable premium was charged over the ordinary first-class train fare, the cost of the air tickets initially being £3 single and £5 return, but in mid-May they were cut by about a third, although the single fare from Plymouth to Torquay or Teignmouth was actually halved to 12s 6d (62½p). Mail was also carried from 15 May, on the same general arrangements as the ordinary rail letter post, with a 3d (1.25p) GWR Air Mail stamp being required in addition to the postage of 1½d (0.625p) for an ordinary inland letter at that time.

The route chosen was not really likely to result in any great queue of passengers. Industry in South Wales was not particularly flourishing, and the Royal Navy had ceased to burn coal. It was thus not much of a surprise when the route was extended at the end of May to include Birmingham. In view of the greater distances involved, the aircraft only did one round trip a day, with almost three hours spent on the ground at Plymouth. The city centre-city centre time for the Birmingham-Cardiff section was 1 hour 55 minutes, which was only about half an hour faster than the streamlined railcar timings when they were subsequently introduced. However the original plan to terminate the services on 12 September was changed 'owing to the large number of passengers using the Birmingham-Cardiff-Torquay-Plymouth air service', and they continued throughout September before following the widespread contemporary practice of shutting down for the winter. A total of 714 passengers was carried during the Great Western's isolated air venture, together with four hundredweight of mail and just over 100 pounds of freight. As the services operated seven days a week, over 400 flights were carried out, so the average loading was well under two passengers per flight – in a six-seater aircraft. The venture lost the GWR £6,500, the costs of the operation being five times the receipts. So, even if aircraft had flown with all six seats filled on every occasion, the revenue would still not have equalled the expenditure incurred.

In March 1934 the combined air services organisation was formally set up by the British railways under the title Railway Air Services Ltd. Although the company was an equal partnership between the four groups and Imperial Airways, the finances of any particular route were the responsibility of the sponsoring railway. Thus in May 1934 the Great Western was back in operation again with a DH84 hired from De Havillands, on a further-extended route which now included Liverpool at the northern end. This was followed in July by a GWR–SR service from Birmingham to Cowes via Bristol and Southampton. The Liverpool service was not particularly popular, only fifty-nine passengers using it in June, but the load factor on the joint GWR–SR route was somewhat better during the high-summer period when it operated. The GWR, however, managed to reduce its actual losses compared with the previous year.

During the remainder of the 1930s there were frequent changes of routes and timetables in the quest of better patronage and financial returns. There were also changes with the structure of the operating companies, 1939 seeing the formation of the 'Great Western & Southern Air Lines – in conjunction with Railway Air Services and Olley Air Services'. This regrouping was perhaps understandable when it is realised that in 1938 the GWR's receipts from their own transport operations were only £905 and they still lost £3,900 on the summer's operation. The rights for internal airline routes in Britain have always been as fiercely contested as were the rival railway schemes during the 'mania'. Those railways that were constructed, however, made a permanent line across the countryside, which, even if they were later abandoned, still left detectable earthworks and other structures that survived for more than the next half a century. Not so the airlines, whose aircraft left no lasting marks in the sky and even on the ground only paid charges for the use of an airfield that was rarely, if ever, actually owned by them. So in the present context there is little to be gained by chronicling the railway air services in detail. Those who are interested should consult John King's paper on the Railway Air Services generally, read to the Royal Aeronautical Society's Historical Group in January 1983 and subsequently published in their *Aerospace*.

Reference should, however, be made to one other facet of the railway's air operations. As with the road services after the formation of the associated companies, the railways generally started to lean on their agencies not to sell tickets for any air services not directly associated with them. The move was far more controversial than had been the case with the buses, and questions started being asked in Parliament. More than twenty of these were tabled over the five years from 1934, and the controversy was aired in the media as well. What was more serious was that the MPs concerned about the matter blocked the railway companies' private railway bills in the House of Commons. Finally the railways' prohibition on agencies was formally stopped in 1938 by an order issued under the 1936 Air Navigation Act. Again John King's 1983 paper gives far more detail of what went on, but the outcome of all the manoeuvring was that the British railway companies finished up with at least a finger in the airline pie, which they would in theory be able to use either for direct profit or to protect their traditional services, depending on how the new form of transport developed.

9

The 1938 Electrification Proposals

In February 1938 considerable interest was aroused by the Great Western's announcement that it had appointed a well-known firm of consulting engineers to prepare a scheme for the electrification of part of the system. The reason for this was the increasing cost of steam working, and it was hoped that 'the substitution of electric traction might enable considerable economies to be effected'. The matter was discussed at some length during the company's Annual Meeting that year, the Chairman, Lord Horne saying that they had been concerned at the upward trend of coal prices. While it was obvious that the railway and the coalfields were involved closely together, there was a limit to what the railway could afford to pay, since every extra shilling (5p) on the cost of coal increased their annual fuel bill by over £100,000 per annum.

The section under consideration for electrification was the main line west of Taunton, which 'although not one over which electrical working is likely to give such good results as in a suburban area, is undoubtedly the most suitable for an immediate purpose, as it readily lends itself to further extensions if the experiment proves to be successful'. There was some

opposition from the shareholders, a member of the British Railway Stockholders Union Ltd claiming that the Southern Railway was at that time curtailing its electrification programme. That railway was in fact still engaged on completing the Mid-Sussex electrification, which was followed by the Gillingham and Maidstone scheme which only came into full operation just before war was declared. It was the start of hostilities that actually stopped work on the construction of the completely new railway from Motspur Park beyond Chessington South, which was electrified from the outset.

What was clear was that the cost of coal at the pithead was rising rapidly. From an average price of 12s 11d (64½p) per ton in 1934, it had only increased to 13s (65p) in the following year, while 1936 saw the figure rise to 14s (70p), and in the third quarter of 1937 to no less than 17s 1½d (86½p). These were the overall averages for all grades of fuel, and the prime steam coal was well above this price. In January 1938 the selling price for 'Large Steam Coal for Export' was 25s (£1.25) f.o.b. (Free on Board) in the South Wales Docks, having been transported and loaded by the Great Western.

The engineers appointed to prepare the electrification scheme were the well-known firm of Merz & McLellan, who had been so closely associated with the original Tyneside suburban scheme of 1904, as well as the North Eastern's proposal to electrify their main line from Newcastle to York. Their resulting report, dated February 1939, is a most interesting document. There is a copy in the Library of the National Railway Museum, marked 'Private and Confidential', although the main conclusions were actually published very quickly by the GWR.

After a preliminary examination of the various lines west of Taunton, it was decided that the study should cover the following:

1. The Main line Taunton to Penzance
2. The Kingswear Branch, including the line to Brixham
3. The Par-Newquay Branch
4. The Cornwall mineral lines
5. The Par-Fowey-Lostwithiel loop line

In 1932 an order by the Minister of Transport, following the Weir Report of 1931 on 'Main Line Railway Electrification', stipulated that future British electrification should use direct current, either from a third rail at 750 volts or from a 1500-volt overhead line, although, with the Minister's express consent, 3,000 volts could be used in the latter instance. For the West of England scheme, an examination of the alternative overhead alternatives showed that there would be an overall reduction in cost of nearly £½ million by adopting the higher voltage, the lower capital expenditure on the supply system well outweighing the added expense of the higher-voltage locomotives.

Some very interesting points come to light in the report. Although the catenary was to start at Taunton, the operators did not propose to stop any trains there specially to change from steam to electric traction or vice versa. As a result of this, certain services would have continued to Exeter, Newton Abbot or even Plymouth with steam locomotives 'under the wires'. Even so, there would have been great activity at Taunton with change-overs, particularly on summer Saturdays and during the Christmas Eve peak. The study determined that in one period of six hours there would be sixty additional light-engine movements through the station, with the complication of having to turn the steam locomotives somewhere, while thirty-four main-line services passed through in the same period without stopping, and a further ten trains arrived or departed over the Barnstaple and Minehead branches. The brief given the consultants clearly stipulated that they were to work to the existing timetables, with no alterations in the average speeds of trains of all classes. The report mentioned that some improvement would be possible because of the higher starting acceleration and increased speeds up gradients, and hazarded the opinion that it would be feasible to speed up a few selected trains, such as the 'Cornish Riviera Express', by about twenty minutes between Taunton and Penzance. The 'Western' and Class 50 diesels, with appreciably less drawbar horsepower than the most powerful electric proposed in 1939, showed that it was easily possible to cut the schedules by more than this in the 1960s and 1970s. The report thus makes no allowance for any additional revenue from a larger number of passengers attracted to the faster trains. The proposed economies resulted very largely from the ability to do away with assistant locomotives on passenger trains, although the strength of wagon draw-bars still required the heaviest freight trains to be banked in places. Single manning of all locomotives was assumed, a state of affairs that was to require a further two decades or so to attain on our main lines.

Four different types of locomotive were proposed, all to be fitted with nose-suspended motors. The most powerful were to be the eight Class 1–Co+Co–1s, with a one-hour rating of 2,550 horsepower. From the status point of view, these were the electrical counterparts of the Kings, with a maximum drawbar pull of 45,000 lb and a total weight of 140 tons. However, with a maximum axle loading of only nineteen tons, they ought to have got across Saltash Bridge, which would have been an advantage. They would not have been all that dissimilar to a 50 per cent more powerful version of the Southern main-line diesel-electrics of 1951, or, indeed, of the BR class 40s that appeared seven years later still. Moving further down the scale, there were to be forty class II and fifty-five class IIa locomotives. They were stated to be similar in general design to the class Is, but of lower power. The class IIs would have weighed 122 tons, and would have had six motors with an aggregate horsepower of 2,100, but the smaller class IIas were to have had only four such motors. As they only turned the scales at ninety tons, they were presumably of the 1–Bo+Bo–1 layout. These two classes might respectively be considered as the electrical counterparts of the Castles and the 2–6–0s. Finally there were to have been sixty-one class III 'four-axle' locomotives (presumably Bo–Bos) for 'small local trains, ballast and other departmental trains, banking slow freight trains when necessary, and shunting in goods yards, and banking some of the steam hauled trains in the electrified area'. Even the class Is were only designed for a maximum speed of 75 mph, although 80 mph was then the general limit between Taunton and Newton Abbot, with line speeds of 60 mph from the latter to Plymouth and 55 beyond. The Western Region's civil engineers have clearly done well to permit today's significantly higher speeds on all these stretches.

Broadly-speaking, railway electrification is a proposition where traffic is either heavy or the terrain is such that the superior performance of electrics in the lower speed ranges gives operating advantages, particularly if the electricity can be obtained locally from some convenient hydro-electric power station. While there were indeed such generating systems in Devon, their capacity was nowhere sufficient for any railway electrification supply. The relatively low operating costs for electric traction mean that it is economic to stimulate off-peak traffic by a frequent service of trains, usually of a regular-interval nature, but, as already mentioned, no such changes were assumed in the brief given to Merz & McLellan. Indeed, the reverse actually applied, because in order to meet the peak services in the summer and at Christmas, the capital cost for the whole scheme was considerably increased, due to the extra locomotives required, coupled with the additional equipment necessary to supply the electrical power that was needed.

Even with the optimistic manning levels assumed, the proposed changes would have given a saving of only £100,500 per annum, while the total capital costs of the four-year electrification scheme would have come to £4,361,100. After deducting a mere 1½ per cent per annum for depreciation, the net annual savings came to less than £33,000, representing a return of 0.75 per cent on the capital outlay. Even with a bank rate of only 2 per cent, there was thus clearly no case for electrification. By contrast, when Merz & McLellan did a study on the LNER in 1930, they estimated a return of over 7 per cent from electrifying the former GNR main lines, an important difference being, in the consulting engineers' view, the factor of the peaks. Having reached this conclusion, they briefly considered the possibility of confining the electrification to the Taunton-Plymouth

58. If the Great Western had electrified its lines west of Taunton, double heading of heavy passenger trains over the South Devon banks would have become a thing of the past. Mogul no 5398 pilots no 6016, 'King Edward V', at the head of a down train climbing Dainton Bank in 1939.

stretch, together with the Kingswear branch, but the overall result was the same.

In retrospect there are a number of surprises as well as a lot of interesting figures in the report. The two-mile branch from Churston to Brixham was never exactly a passenger money-

spinner. In the 1926 *Report on Branch Lines* the passenger revenue was given as only £6,120 out of a total of nearly £26,000. Total operating costs were then £7,408. There was a fairly frequent auto-train service, and this would perhaps have been replaced by an electric multiple-unit, as proposed for the Plymouth suburban services, but even so there were still the frequent competitive buses around Torbay, operated by the associated Devon General company. One would be hard put to it to find many branches of such length throughout the world that have ever been electrified, although the LNER's Woodhead scheme, being planned at the same time, included the even-shorter line from Dinting to Glossop. That does serve part of the commuting area of one of our largest cities, where today the ability of the multiple units to reverse at frequent intervals enables them to make an important contribution to the Greater Manchester transport system.

Another surprising inclusion was the proposal to install the wires along the Cornish china clay branches. Electrifying the line from Par to Newquay made sense from the point of view of operating passenger trains over the steeply-graded single-track sections, particularly during the summer when a pair of 4–6–0s on the front of the Paddington-Newquay trains would still require the assistance of a 2–6–2T at the rear up the bank to Luxulyan. One can hardly imagine it could have been economic to have electric locomotives shunting the 'drys' on the mineral branches and working the unfitted wagons to and from the concentration yards at St Blazey. It made more sense to consider electrifying the line from there to Fowey, and the guards of steam trains threading their way through the confines of Pinnock Tunnel would have relished the clearer atmosphere. It might, however, have been difficult to obtain the necessary clearances for 3,000 volt wires in the single-bore tunnel, which is the longest in Cornwall. The use of electric traction over a trunk mineral route between one concentration yard and another had been tried in the North-East, when the line from Shildon to Newport was electrified in 1915. There, over a much longer route, five electric locomotives were said by Sir Vincent Raven to do the work of thirteen steam ones, but the quantity of coal carried was considerably greater than the 685, 696 tons of clay handled at Fowey

in 1937. Changed patterns of mining in Durham and the construction of larger steelworks on Teesside made that scheme less attractive as the years passed, and when expensive renewals of some of the electrification equipment became necessary, the line reverted to steam traction in 1935.

Another somewhat surprising feature of the 1939 report is the level of charges assumed for depreciation. An annual figure of just over 1½ per cent was applied not only to the electrical supply equipment, but to the locomotives as well. That appears to infer a life of about sixty years, so that, if we take it at its face value, had the scheme progressed, the original electric locomotives would still, at the time of writing, have another twenty years' service in front of them. In the Weir Committee's 1934 report details were given of two schemes examined by Merz & McLellan. The one for the LNER assumed a depreciation rate of 3½ per cent for the electric locomotives, but less than half of one per cent for the electrification equipment, and the corresponding figures for the LMS Crewe-Carlisle proposals were very similar. The accounting procedure adopted in the case of the GWR proposal was actually on a sinking fund basis, with a sum of money being put into the fund each year to accumulate at a compound interest of 3 per cent.

Because steam heating was in universal use on the Great Western's coaching stock in 1938, it would have been necessary to provide some means of steam generation on the locomotives used for passenger haulage. It was considered that the best way of doing this would have been in oil-fired boilers on the locomotives, the cost of energy being significantly higher if electric power were used. In the light of post-World War II experience on British Railways, the reliability of such oil-fired boilers left much to be desired, and they still in the 1980s require the services of a second man, although it should be recorded that the Danish State Railways have one-man operation of their remaining locomotives equipped with boilers of that type.

Reference was made earlier to the fact that it was assumed that the electric locomotives would be single-manned. While, as already mentioned, it took until the 1960s to achieve single-manning on main-line electric and diesel locomotives, it is at least possible to imagine that, under the economic conditions at the end of the 1930s, the staff would have accepted such an arrangement. The GWR had brought it in for its streamlined railcars, even when working routes such as that between Birmingham and Cardiff. If the GWR had proceeded with its electrification, and had successfully established the concept of single-manning, the general profitability of our main lines would have improved markedly once the new motive power provided under the 1955 modernisation plan had come into operation.

The proposal to construct locomotives of the 1–Co+Co–1 type was somewhat surprising. Despite the start of World War II, Gresley's first electric locomotive for the Woodhead route appeared in 1941. This packed 1,870 horsepower into an 88-ton machine carried on two four-wheel bogies, and the stretched Co–Co version, which did not actually appear until the scheme had been restarted after World War II, had a rating of 2,490 horsepower. Some of the latter are incidentally, at the time of writing, still at work in Holland, thirty years after building, having been sold following the withdrawal of passenger services over Woodhead. These two designs were equipped with regenerative braking, which was of considerable help when working heavy unfitted freight trains over the Pennines. Merz & McLellan decided against the provision of such equipment for the Taunton-Penzance scheme on the grounds that the energy

recovered would not be sufficient to justify the extra cost and the increased maintenance of the locomotives. This was entirely consistent with the general philosophy for the whole proposal that the existing operating practices should not be altered. One cannot but agree that the energy recovery would not have been very great financially. However, comments I have had from drivers in the West of England in recent years leave no doubt that the benefits of a better braking system than the standard vacuum one are very considerable on the switchbacks of the former Great Western main line in Devon and Cornwall.

As already mentioned, the economics of the scheme were not attractive, and even to this day the Western Region remains the only one in the country without any electric traction. So ostensibly the study by Merz & McLellan was entirely wasted. The total expenditure by the Weir Committee's report eight years earlier had been £5,456 and that included the costs of the two investigations carried out by Merz & McLellan at the Committee's request on schemes for the LMS and LNER. It seems unlikely therefore that the GWR spent much more than £2,000 commissioning their report. However, when one studies the subject of electrification in more detail it is surprising that the Great Western even went to this expense at the beginning of 1938. Seven years earlier the Weir report had referred to the fact that the GWR had already investigated the economic possibilities of electrifying the Taunton-Penzance section of its main line, but had not proceeded with it. One would hardly think it necessary to call in consultants to up-date a previous report. This, coupled with certain aspects of the brief already referred to, makes it very obvious that the whole exercise was directed at a totally different end.

Another consideration reinforces this conclusion. Throughout the inter-war years, the GWR had demonstrated time and again how conscious it was of the publicity and increased patronage resulting from the acceleration of train services. It is thus inconceivable that in any serious appraisal of the advantages of electrification they would not have taken full advantage of the superior speed potential. To have done so, however, would have required a very considerable input of effort by the railway's own staff to determine the new schedules and rosters, and to estimate the effect on passenger revenues and costs. To give the consultants all the existing documentation and tell them just to work from that was a much simpler operation for all concerned at Swindon and Paddington, and this would have minimised the total resources committed to the study.

It thus seems very clear that there was some other reason for commissioning the study. One could imagine that it was a publicity move, because the announcement certainly caught the public's imagination. As a youngster of eleven living in the West Country, I was aware of the proposals. However, all the evidence points to it being a device to bring pressure on the collieries to ensure that they did not push the cost of their coal too high. Lord Horne had spelt out the threat to the coal owners quite clearly at the 1938 Annual Meeting, and it is interesting to note that what started as an instruction 'to prepare a scheme for the electrification of part of our system' had, a year later, become 'a detailed investigation into the possibility of electrifying the Taunton–Penzance section'. What had happened therefore in the interim? The answer was that coal prices had fallen. Already by the end of April 1938 the f.o.b. price of export steam coal in South Wales had dropped 1s 6d (7½p) per ton from its January level. By July it stabilised at 23s (£1.15) which was maintained up to the time at which the gathering war-clouds resulted in the suspension of that particular return to the Board of Trade in April 1939. Merz & McLellan did not even refer in their report to the prices for coal that had been assumed in their costing studies, although they stated that the figures represented the present-day costs including recent increases in wages, price of coal, etc. On the figures originally given by Lord Horne, a drop of 2s (10p) per ton was worth nearly £¼ million per annum to the GWR. When studying any past economic trends, it is impossible to be dogmatic in ascribing cause and effect, but there are very strong indications from the above evidence that the return on the Great Western's expenditure on its electrification study resulted in it being one of the most profitable business investments ever made.

10
A Review of the 1930s

When it comes to taking an over-view of the Great Western's activities in the 1930s, it is useful to use as a starting point the recommendations of the Royal Commission on Transport. Their third report, as summarised by the GWR in February 1931, contained nine major recommendations, and we can review their performance over the rest of the decade in the light of these specific points.

1. Rail services should be speeded up and made more convenient. In these days of hourly Inter-City 125 services from London to Bristol and Swansea, no-one could argue with the advantages of such services, but this particular recommendation of the Royal Commission must have relied heavily on the lead already taken by the GWR in achieving average speeds in the upper sixties with the steam-hauled 'Cheltenham Flyer'. We have already discussed the ultimate achievements with that train, but they only represented a fraction of the total improvements that took place with the speeding-up of services throughout the 1930s. While the Great Western was to lose its records to other British railways in the fields of maximum and average speeds, the average GWR passenger nevertheless benefited very considerably during the 1930s from the general speeding-up.

2. Revision and lowering of fares would assist in the recovery of traffic. Reducing fares is always a gamble, necessitating a proportionate increase in traffic just to compensate for the lost revenue, while the physical resources may not be available to meet the new peaks that result. The railways as a whole maintained a common approach on fares, and throughout the 1930s there was a general downward trend, culminating in the adoption of the monthly return in 1933. This was based on a fare-plus-a-third for return journeys, which for third-class travellers worked out at the old figure of 1d per mile (.42p per mile) laid down in the days of the Victorian Regulation of the Railways Acts. The only difference was that in the 1930s they were available 'by all trains without exception', rather than on the 'Parley' all-stations trains that just managed to achieve the minimum speeds laid down by law. To begin with, these fares were only available during the summer months, but from 1935 they became universal. As a result of these fare changes and other activities, the number of passengers carried by the GWR increased by some 6 per cent between 1933 and 1937, but were all virtually lost in the downturn of the following year. Passenger receipts, however, did rather better, rising by 13 per cent to 1937, and then dropping back only marginally in 1938. There was a general rise of 5 per cent in all railway charges in the autumn of 1937, except for passenger fares in the London area, where they were only similarly increased in the summer of 1939.

3. *Statutory obligation should be placed on rail-way companies to provide a seat for each passenger journey on a main-line train at its starting point.* The obligation for any *statutory* change clearly lies with Parliament, and this recommendation has never, to this day, been incorporated into legislation. Nevertheless after 1948 British Railway's first set of conditions for the issue of passenger tickets laid it down that if anyone could not obtain a seat of the appropriate class on any particular train, the full fare would be immediately refunded at the booking office. The recommendation anyway has a strong bias towards the London resident, and so may not have had quite the nationwide appeal that the Royal Commission imagined. The GWR, like the other railway companies, certainly developed its seat reservation facilities during the 1930s, the number of individual operations increasing from just over a quarter of a million in 1929 to over 423,000 in 1938 and went to great lengths to regulate the loading of its summer Saturday trains out of Paddington.

4. *Joint or overlapping lines should be merged into one or other of the groups.* Such rationalisation only occurred some years after nationalisation, and even thirty years later critics of British Railway's locomotive manning practices claim that they are determined by the pre-1948 boundaries. As far as the GWR was concerned, one major 'overlapping' line was the former Midland route to Bristol, and it would have been hard to integrate the services southwestwards from New Street with those to the north of that point. In any case both lines were needed on summer week-ends. It is interesting, however, to speculate what the Great Western might have made of the Somerset & Dorset Joint had the northern portion passed into its control. The former Great Western & Great Central Joint from Northolt to Ashendon formed a useful common route that was relatively lightly loaded by both of the individual owners. It is doubtful if much advantage would have resulted from selling it to one or other of the partners, who were not using it for competing services anyway. Similar considerations applied to the joint GWR–LMS lines in the Welsh border area, but had the Great Western taken control of the Central Wales line, one wonders whether all the LMS services in the Swansea area would have survived the withdrawal of the competition.

5. *All competitive traffic should be pooled.* As we have seen, there were positive overt moves in this direction, and much more went on behind the scenes to foster activities of common interest.

6. *All surburban services should be electrified, not only in London, but elsewhere.* About the only comment that can be made on such a recommendation is 'Hear, Hear!' although perhaps some of the Southern's commuters today might demur in the autumn leaf-fall season or after a snowfall. It was, in fact, only the LNER which took up this point *ab initio* in the late 1930s, with their Liverpool-Shenfield scheme, completion of which was delayed by World War II. The Southern Railway was already by 1931 well into its electrification programme, which was beginning to spread outside the traditional suburban area. In 1983 Paddington still remains the only major London terminus which handles no British Railways electric trains, although electric trains of London Transport still come and go to Hammersmith as they did when the GWR had a

G. H. Soole Collection, National Railway Museum, York

59. The Royal Commission on Transport in the 1930s recommended the elimination of joint and overlapping lines. This never came about but there was still a considerable degree of cooperation as illustrated by this photograph of the northbound 'Devonian' leaving Bristol in the late 1930s. It is hauled by LMS Jubilee no 5609 'Gilbert and Ellice Islands', but the rear four coaches are Great Western ones.

& Altrincham, the LMS Wirral scheme, the LNER's South Tyneside route, and the replacement of rope haulage on the Glasgow Underground.

half-share in the Hammersmith & City rolling stock from 1906 onwards.

Away from the capital city, there was nothing more than moderate activity following this particular recommendation of the Royal Commission, the only electrifications carried out in the 1930s being the Manchester, South Junction

7.   *Greater encouragement should be extended to the use of larger wagons.* The Royal Commission, in coming to this recommendation, referred specifically to the Great Western's lead with their twenty-tonners, but improvement in the 1930s was slow, if only because of the vast number of wagons involved, many of them

60. Greater use of containers was recommended by the Royal Commission on Transport. The photograph shows one of the GWR's furniture removal containers in 1935.

privately owned, pottering their slow and cheap way round the country's rail system.

8. *Containers should be more generally used.* The Great Western was active in this field throughout the 1930s, but the container revolution did not really take off until well after World War II when their use spread to the international shipping scene, and the speeds attainable with air-braked Freightliner trains gave significant operating and commercial advantages.

9. *Financial and statistical returns should be reviewed in order to see whether they can be reduced and simplified.* These were largely statutory in character, and the Ministry of Transport's agreement was thus necessary to cut out any paperwork. It took the pressures of World War II to make any significant inroad into these requirements, as can be seen from examination of the GWR's annual report for 1939, but as late as the 1970s the Derwent Valley Railway had to seek special permission to delete certain returns from its annual report to avoid disclosure of the level of its customers' business activities.

Table 6 RAILWAY DIVIDENDS

Year	GWR (%)	LMS (%)	LNER Preferred (%)	Deferred (%)	SR Preferred (%)	Deferred (%)
1930	5½	2	¼	nil	5	1¼
1931	3	¼	nil	nil	4	nil
1932	3	nil	nil	nil	1	nil
1933	3	nil	nil	nil	3	nil
1934	3	nil	nil	nil	4	nil
1935	3	nil	nil	nil	5	nil
1936	3	1¼	½	nil	5	½
1937	4	1½	1¾	nil	5	1½
1938	½	nil	nil	nil	5	nil
1939	3½	1½	nil	nil	5	1¼

Source: LMS Handbooks of Statistics and Company Annual Reports

It just remains, therefore, to examine the Great Western's financial results for the 1930s, and compare them with those of the other main-line companies, as shown in Table 6. The Great Western was bitterly disappointed that it could not declare any higher dividend than ½ per cent in 1938, the Chairman at the Annual Meeting referring to the fact that 'This decision breaks a proud record of nearly seventy years during which the Great Western Railway dividend has never fallen below 3 per cent'. Bearing in mind the fact that this came from the same speech in which Lord Horne announced the electrification proposals, it is worth considering the financial background in some greater detail. To have raised the dividend to 3 per cent would have cost the company under £1¼ million. While they had appropriated £100,000 from the Contingency Fund of just over £3m, they then carried forward an £87,000 balance into 1939, so effectively only abstracted £13,000 from this account. For the six consecutive years from 1930 to 1935 the GWR only managed to maintain their three per cent annual dividend by apportioning sums of up to £1.35 million from reserves in a single year, with a total of over £4½ million being involved. So it rather looks as if the actions they took in early 1939 were primarily intended to back up the railways' 'Square Deal' campaign, rather than as a result of dire poverty.

Neglecting, or perhaps even commending, this particular aberration, the Great Western's financial performance in the 1930s compared well with those of the other British Railway companies, and was at least half as great again as the bank rate which remained at the two per cent level for virtually the whole decade. But harder times lay ahead for the company and its operations as total war engulfed Britain in the years that followed Hitler's march into Poland.

Index